Pioneer Woman Educator

D1559087

NUMBER FORTY-EIGHT
The Centennial Series
OF THE ASSOCIATION OF FORMER STUDENTS,
Texas A&M

Pioneer Woman Educator

The Progressive Spirit
of
Annie Webb Blanton

Debbie Mauldin Cottrell

Texas A&M University Press
College Station

FRONTISPIECE: Blanton as a professor at the University of Texas
in the late 1920s. (Photo courtesy Barker Texas History Center,
University of Texas, Austin, Photograph Collection.)

The paper used in this book meets the minimum requirements of the
American National Standard for Permanence of Paper for Printed Library
Materials, Z39.48-1984. Binding materials have been chosen for durability.

Library of Congress Cataloging-in-Publication Data

Cottrell, Debbie Mauldin, 1956–
  Pioneer woman educator : the progressive spirit of
Annie Webb Blanton / Debbie Mauldin Cottrell.
      p.   cm. — (Centennial series of the Association
of Former Students, Texas A&M University ; no. 48)
    Includes bibliographical references (p.   ) and index.
    ISBN 0-89096-543-9. — ISBN 0-89096-555-2 (pbk.)
    1. Blanton, Annie Webb, 1870–1945.   2. Educa-
tors—Texas—Biography.   3. Women educators—
Texas—Biography.   4. School superintendents—
Texas—Biography.   I. Title.   II. Series.
LA2317.B544C68   1993
371.1'0092—dc20   93-9375
  [B]   CIP

Everything that helps to wear away age-old prejudices
contributes towards the advancement of women
and of humanity.

—Annie Webb Blanton
May 31, 1922

Contents

Illustrations

Preface

This biography of Annie Webb Blanton grew out of my desire to learn more about a woman for whom an elementary school had been named in a neighborhood near where I grew up in Dallas. When as an adult in Austin, I attempted to locate more details on this name long familiar to me, I discovered that no full account of her existed.[1] More out of curiosity than as a well-planned effort, I began my own search to learn about Blanton, her accomplishments, and the reason why no one had previously undertaken her life history. Several years later, my search has culminated in this volume.

My research on Blanton took me across Texas and led me to memorable people and places. However, two experiences—one early in my work and the other which unfolded as I completed this book—strike me as indicative of the realities one encounters when attempting to deal with women's contributions to history.

I made an early research trip to the University of North Texas in Denton, where Blanton lived and taught for seventeen years, established her educational and political credentials, and based her campaigns for state superintendent and for Congress. While there, I asked a professor and historian of the school to explain how current faculty and students viewed Blanton and how she was portrayed to them through history. His answer was direct: hardly anyone on campus would recognize her name, there was no special tribute to her anywhere in Denton, and most, if not all, physical evidence of her time in Denton was long destroyed. While not shocking or necessarily suggesting overt antifemale sentiments, this news was still telling, and I remember wondering just what a woman in early twentieth-century Texas would have to have accomplished to avoid obliteration in her adopted hometown.

In 1990 and 1991, toward the end of this project, I participated in and observed the effort led by the Texas Historical Commission to have a state office building in Austin named for Blanton, a symbolic gesture but one that I knew could encourage the important process of historical inquiry. This episode, unlike the one in Denton, has been more difficult to attribute to things simply overlooked or forgotten. Blanton's contributions to state government were not questioned, but her worthiness to join the male-dominated roster of building names in Austin was rigorously scrutinized. Some opponents to the naming questioned how significant it was that she was merely the first woman to achieve certain levels in education and politics (implying, I think, that getting there is not necessarily important, although these opponents conceded that what she did after that was noteworthy). Others suggested that only a building housing education offices should bear her name, a requirement not previously made for male candidates. Some argued that the building be named instead for the immediate past governor of the state, presumably a "safer" choice all around. And, at the end of the debate, this was the choice the state endorsed. Whatever their reasons and political persuasions, it is clear that, when given the opportunity to expose the public to an important woman in Texas history, many individuals currently involved in state government hesitated and expressed an age-old reservation.[2]

I am not sure that Blanton would much care about either of these issues, and they certainly do not represent the only times I encountered obscurity or lost evidence regarding her. Nevertheless, they form interesting bookends for this historical study and remind me of the context in which works such as this are sometimes received. In many ways, Blanton represents to me an elite figure in Texas and women's history, and I cannot pretend to offer this work as history from the bottom up. Yet in a larger sense, apparently, Blanton has not been considered elite enough to be remembered in the most basic ways.

In this book I hope to provide an in-depth, balanced study of a woman who achieved undeniable distinction in the educational history of Texas. Moving beyond what she accomplished, I analyze what motivated her and allowed her to rise from the classroom to become a significant leader in the state's progressive movement. Imposing modern-day or ahistorical values on the past is an inherent risk in this type of study, and one I hope to have avoided here. Thus, rather than seeking to use a strict yardstick to measure the successes or failures of Blanton, I attempt to determine *why* Blanton became and accomplished what she did, *how* she got where she did, *what* she did with her opportunities, and *why* it was Blanton and not someone else who did all this. The framework for my analysis places Blanton's life in the context of both women's studies and educational history. Even though her personal papers do not appear to have survived intact, many of Blanton's letters and other written materials reside in the collections of educators, suffragists, and other colleagues and friends. Using these records I attempt to provide a full-length biography of Blanton, though the nature of the available research material has necessitated an emphasis on her public life.

Even while I wrote this book, education in Texas dominated the news as state officials sought a more equitable funding system for schools. The lengthy battles, the endless legislative sessions, the concerns of the poor, and the fears of the wealthy provided a constant reminder that educational reform is never an easy task.[3] Scholarship on the women of Texas history remains in a relatively nascent stage of development, and thus we are, perhaps unfortunately, still completing basic exploration on an upper echelon of women who contributed to the state's history. This book reflects that situation, but I offer it with the hope that an analysis of Annie Webb Blanton's life will contribute to a broader, more comprehensive understanding of both women in Texas history and the state's educational heritage.

Acknowledgments

I wish to express my appreciation to the staffs of several libraries, including the Barker Texas History Center at the University of Texas, Austin; the Houston Metropolitan Research Center; the Texas Collection at Baylor University, Waco; the Texas State Library, Austin; the Austin History Center; the University of North Texas Archives, Denton; and the Texas Woman's University Library, Denton. Ralph Elder at Barker and Peg Rezac at TWU were particularly helpful.

My thanks go to the journal *Locus* for allowing me to incorporate into this work my article "Politics and Education: The Career of Annie Webb Blanton, 1918–1922," which was published in their Fall 1990 issue. Another version of chapter 5 of this book appeared as "Professional, Feminine, and Feminist: Annie Webb Blanton and the Founding of Delta Kappa Gamma," in *Women and Texas History: Selected Essays* (Texas State Historical Association, 1993), with the mutual consent of my friends at TSHA and the Texas A&M University Press.

Many members and chapters of Delta Kappa Gamma have been especially encouraging about a scholarly study of Annie Webb Blanton's life and have provided several opportunities for me to try ideas, ask questions, and meet others with helpful information. A special thanks in this respect goes to Betty Wright of Cleburne, who put me in touch with numerous excellent sources. I also am grateful to those friends, former students, and family members of Blanton's, many of whom are also affiliated with Delta Kappa Gamma, who shared their memories of her with me.

The idea for turning my interest in Blanton into a book germinated while I was employed by the Texas Historical Commission, and many friends there provided the initial encouragement essential to making such an undertaking a reality. Particular gratitude goes to Cynthia Beeman, Roni Morales, Frances Rickard, Jim Steely, and Curtis Tunnell for their ideas, indulgence, and consistent belief in this work. When the project led me to graduate school at the University of Texas at Austin, I again found encouragement and good spirit on many fronts. Professors Lewis Gould and Susan Glenn provided their expertise and knowledge to my Master's thesis (from which this book is derived) in numerous and wise ways, and to them I extend both my professional and personal appreciation. I also want to thank Noel Parsons and Camille North at Texas A&M University Press for their assistance. Although I never officially sat in their classrooms, I have learned a great deal from Betty and Will Lowrance, who have long exemplified to me the best in the teaching profession. Both their knowledge and their friendship have influenced this work. Alan Cottrell has provided the perfect blend of believing in my work while challenging me to make it better, and more than anyone else has tolerantly (sometimes even enthusiastically) endured the creation of this work. Finally, I dedicate this book to my parents, who offered me love, support, security, and educational opportunities, which directly affected my desire and ability to study the life of Annie Webb Blanton.

Although each of these individuals contributed significantly to this work, the interpretations and conclusions reached here, including any mistakes or shortcomings, are solely my own.

Introduction

In 1918 Annie Webb Blanton broke the gender barrier in Texas politics when she was elected to head the state's public school system. This victory came despite the fact that women in Texas could not vote in the general election that elevated her to office. Yet by using their recently attained right to vote in primaries and joining with prohibition forces and opponents of former governor James E. Ferguson, white women had played a pivotal role a few months earlier in getting Blanton onto the final November ballot as the Democratic candidate for state superintendent of public instruction. Once there, she was easily swept into office, becoming the first woman elected to a statewide political position. As proponents of suffrage had argued, attaining primary voting rights was a starting point for bringing women into the electorate, and in a predominantly one-party state such as Texas, they could prove influential.

Blanton's victory was indeed decisive for the suffrage movement in Texas, as it worked towards full enfranchisement of women at the state and national levels. Yet her election cannot be completely understood in terms of suffrage politics alone. Had she not possessed an unwavering commitment to improving Texas schools and women's status in the teaching profession, Blanton would have neither embraced the suffrage movement in Texas nor entered the political arena. The motivation behind her commitment to these causes and the way she chose to define and carry out her work are crucial for understanding both Blanton and the social and political nuances of Progressive-era Texas.

Blanton based her career as politician and professional educator on a unique blend of southern traditionalism, reform feminism, and purposeful Progressivism. In many ways, she projected the typical image of an early twentieth-century schoolteacher — always properly dressed, her long hair pulled back in an elaborate bun, and demonstrating a strong sense of responsibility and duty, characterized by the rather no-nonsense manner she brought to whatever task she undertook. She thrived on work, and with her own industrious and bright approach, she used her tenacity to her advantage as few before her had. Blanton was no great wit, no sterling writer; at times she could be intolerant and prudish. Still, she was unselfish and determined to arrange her life so that whatever she accomplished would extend beyond her own personal gain. A sense of femininity undergirded her personality, and she took no offense at being perceived as a "southern lady." Yet, if Blanton comfortably accepted the traditional notion that women were different from men, she adamantly fought against the prevalent idea that different meant inferior. In fact, Blanton believed that women — particularly those of her own race, social and economic class, and profession — were capable of improving society and reforming schools as well as, if not better than, many men. This belief shaped her Progressivism and influenced her lifelong fight for better schools in Texas.

Blanton's ascent as a leader among Texas educators officially began with her election as president of the Texas State Teachers Association in 1916. From that position her prominence grew. She subsequently served four years as state superintendent of public instruction; established a career as a professor of education at the University of Texas, where she became an expert in rural education training; and founded what is now an international society for women educators, Delta Kappa Gamma. Simultaneous with these accomplishments, Blanton earned graduate degrees, researched and wrote books, and remained an active classroom teacher. She was driven by relentless energy and a sense of the correctness of her convictions, traits that germinated in her as a child of a proud southern family from Houston.

Her educational training and childhood experiences were neither unusual nor special. Like many single young women in the late nineteenth century, she assumed a position as a rural schoolteacher upon graduation from high school. Nevertheless, prior to taking this job Blanton had determined also to earn a college degree, and this decision would eventually distinguish her from most of her female contemporaries and enable her to become a leader in Texas education. In the course of pursuing her intellectual and career goals, Blanton quickly became aware of the discrimination facing women who undertook such endeavors and of the substantial loss of potential such discrimination created. These early experiences inspired her consistent, lifelong effort to unite competent, experienced women teachers in order to fight professional unfairness and to use their talents for society's betterment. The exercise of voting rights and other political involvements were ways to work for such goals, but for Blanton the suffrage movement, in general, and the achievements in her term as state superintendent, in particular, were only two elements of her broader effort to improve Texas schools through the organized utilization of the skills and influences of those women who had already demonstrated their professional competence.

This perspective indicates Blanton's desire to participate in broadening women's emancipation more than by simply increasing women's legal rights, and it speaks to the critical issue of the feminist manifestations in Blanton's life. As contemporary historians of women have noted, applying a label of "feminism" to an individual is a less useful approach of historical analysis than attempting to understand the feminist aspects evident in a given event or individual. Annie Webb Blanton held a clear conviction that male dominance — especially in politics and education — needed challenging and could, in fact, be changed. The mechanism for change, she believed, centered on enlisting strong female leaders who could inspire other women to contribute to improving society. Like many others who rose to public service through the "traditional" female outlets of teaching and participating in women's clubs, Blanton held no startling feminist ideology — it appears that she never used the word "feminist" — but rather found her motivation in a naturally developing awareness of gender inequities. In her own words, she encountered and climbed the "solid wall of sex prejudice" and then spent her life "stretching out [her] hands" to others who could help beat that wall down permanently. Her perception of what women needed to do, and the way she acted on this perception, indicated that Blanton was pro-woman without being anti-man. Without losing sight of gender differences, she recognized the need for rethinking the balance and common ground between the sexes as a means to more effectively reform society. As this volume shows, her commitment to women's issues was tempered, influenced, and complicated by other important tenets in her life, including elitism, racism, and professionalism; however, it nonetheless remained central to her motivations and forms the essential context for understanding Annie Webb Blanton.[1]

Blanton's feminist persuasions derived from her professional experiences, but they came to influence her personal life as well. She surrounded herself with women who shared her own ideas about women's role in education and from whom she drew strength and motivation. Blanton was clearly most comfortable in the company of her own gender—although this did not inhibit her ability to maintain cordial working relationships with male colleagues—especially those who shared her ideas about educational reforms. Blanton's professional relationships with men seem to have been influenced by her own substantial record of achievement and her, in general, non-alienating approach to working for women's causes. Blanton gave the impression of one who sought to improve the system, not to overthrow it, and she found that the Progressive spirit of Texas politics in the early part of this century created a sympathetic environment for her goals and ideals among both men and women.

An analysis of Blanton's life (1870–1945) reveals insights into Progressive-era politics in Texas as seen from the perspective of a feminist educator who had strong ties to traditional southern principles. Concern for the schools of Texas and, especially, for the women in these schools, proved a persistent cause for action throughout Blanton's life. Her pursuit of goals related to these concerns is unparalleled by any other Texan in the twentieth century. Her efforts were often limited—by both the narrow approach she took and the difficulties posed by the educational system and society, even during an era characterized by a reforming spirit—but within these confines she made an indelible mark on Texas history.

Pioneer Woman Educator

The Early Years
1 8 7 0 - 1 9 0 1

In the late 1800s educational policies in Texas and throughout the southern part of the United States were in a state of flux. Two distinct, controversial issues dominated the course of school development in the region: imposition of and consequent reaction to Reconstruction policies, and the broadening of higher educational opportunities. During this period of change, Annie Webb Blanton was born in Houston, on August 19, 1870.[1] Her own future opportunities, career, and ultimate role as the most prominent twentieth-century female educator in the state would be directly affected by the educational situation in Texas at her birth.

The most obvious influence on education in the southern United States of 1870 was the region's ongoing reaction to Reconstruction policies. The Civil War had disrupted the progress of education across the country, but the war's aftermath proved even more damaging as southern states reacted bitterly to newly centralized state school systems, which Reconstruction governments imposed. In Texas, such a system began to operate in 1871 and included a common curriculum for all schools, a policy of compulsory attendance, graded class levels, standard teacher certification requirements, and a centralized state board of education, which consisted of the governor, attorney general, and superintendent of public instruction.[2] For the Reconstruction Republicans in control of the state, the new system was a vast improvement over Texas' previous underfunded, decentralized public facilities and its preponderance of private institutions, many of which struggled merely to survive. The Republicans believed their policies would help change the assessment of Texas made by the National Bureau of Education in 1870 as "the darkest field educationally in the United States."³

Yet in Texas and across the South, these Republican goals — intended to establish an educational system for all citizens, not just whites — collided with long-held racial prejudices. Few white southerners approved of having their taxes used to support schools for blacks, a race most of them were not eager to see educated. Related to these concerns, traditional southerners were also suspicious of any state-enforced education system as potentially threatening to their social order. Texans voted Republicans out of office by 1876, and ruling Democrats, eager to undo their predecessors' influence, used the state's new constitution to replace the progressive system with a decentralized program of local schools. This action reflected Texans' disdain for a number of Reconstruction themes: a powerful central governmental authority, a mandate to include opportunities for blacks in educational development, and increased taxation, which the Democrats always feared would become excessive. What resulted from the Democrats' return to power and adoption of the Constitution of 1876 was a community school system in which no local taxes could be collected, no permanent organization existed, small and inefficient schools often operated in place of one larger institution, and facilities routinely faced annual changes in funding, location, and governing boards. The new constitution eliminated compulsory education and mandated segregation of schools. It is not surprising that by the end of the 1870s Texas public schools had seen a decrease in student population, regular attendance, teacher salaries, and overall expenditures per pupil. In 1884, the problems of this system finally resulted in the rewriting of state school laws to allow a more centralized approach, which included the election of a state superintendent to supervise all schools and the authorization of state and local taxes to fund schools. The state made these changes cautiously, however, barely beginning to address the problems in Texas education. It would be well into the twentieth century — when reform-minded educators such as Annie Webb Blanton gained positions of authority — before Texas achieved more extensive reforms and curbed the problems created by anti-Republican reactionaries.[4]

Blanton herself would not have risen to face the challenges of reforming Texas schools in the twentieth century without another educational development that had unfolded in her youth: the broadening of higher educational opportunities, including the increasing place for women in such facilities. Although women in the United States had been first allowed an entrance into higher education when Oberlin College in Ohio became coeducational in 1837, it took the outbreak of the Civil War and consequent depletion of male students to substantially advance women's enrollment in colleges and universities across the country. Even with the opportunity the war created, most women found the greatest encouragement to study not in coeducational schools but in the newly instituted women's colleges in the eastern part of the United States. However, the Morrill Land Grant Act of 1862 aided in establishing state universities and land-grant institutions throughout the country, and their expansive curricula were geared to encouraging college study for a broad range of citizens. These changes in higher education, along with the creation of increasing numbers of teacher training schools, had the general effect of removing the collegiate experience from the domain of the elite, and thus increased opportunities for more women. Southern women, in particular, and especially those whose families were not wealthy, benefited, as possibilities of attending college closer to home opened new doors for them. In 1870, the year Annie Webb Blanton was born, 21 percent of the total undergraduate enrollment in the United States was female; the proportion jumped to 32 percent in 1880 and 40 percent in 1910.[5]

The increased opportunities for women in higher education naturally led to a greater potential for professional advancement than had previously existed. Perhaps more important than specific job opportunities was the general association college-educated women had with the public. As the Progressive era unfolded early in the twentieth century, college-educated women often became leaders in the temperance and suffrage movements and settlement house work, as well as in traditional women's clubs, which increasingly became politicized.[6]

Annie Webb Blanton's life illustrates the common experiences of those southern women who overcame their region's educational problems, seized the opportunities for higher education, and subsequently became educational reformers aligned with progressive elements of southern politics. In many respects Blanton's career even parallels those of female educators at the elite eastern women's colleges: she was single but rarely alone, inherited her family's belief in using her life to contribute to society, saw herself as a pioneer in many of her educational activities, and chose to surround herself with other successful women for emotional and professional support. However, the changing times, the new opportunities, and Blanton's own ultimately successful career should not obscure the difficulties and challenges that remained for any woman who chose to pursue a college degree, especially if she came from a middle-class family, as Blanton did. Even though college enrollments included an increasing percentage of women students in the latter part of the nineteenth century, the overall proportion of the nation's female population aged eighteen to twenty-one that attended college in 1890 was still only 2 percent. Furthermore, the fear that higher education would distract women from domestic roles as wives and mothers remained pervasive in society. Only the most dedicated and determined women steered their lives in the direction of college.[7]

Blanton clearly possessed such determination, though it is difficult to assess its exact origins. Her large family was financially comfortable, but her parents were far from wealthy enough to pay to send their seven children to college. The family also maintained a strong adherence to traditional southern principles, which included a belief in women's responsibility to family and domesticity. This belief, coupled with the deaths of both her mother and twin sister before Blanton graduated from high school, easily could have extinguished any career aspirations she had. In fact, of the three daughters in her family who reached adulthood, she was the only one who chose a professional career over marriage.[8] Thus her background suggested an improbable chance that she would not only receive a university degree, but also go on to earn master's and doctoral degrees, to become both a college professor and Texas' first woman elected to statewide office, and to found a professional society for women teachers.[9]

Yet if Blanton attained her college education and subsequent achievements despite this family background, she also accomplished them without violating the fundamental principles ingrained in her during her formative years. Blanton learned early that hard work was a virtue essential to success, and she practiced this lesson throughout her life. Along with the work ethic, Blanton's family emphasized education and learning, through which individual integrity would be enhanced. In addition, one's relation with society in general was deemed important. The family counted among its ancestors numerous war veterans and politically active citizens, and Blanton was taught that a patriotic duty to one's country necessitated a personal commitment to social concerns. The efforts she later exerted for school reform and increased opportunities for women arose from her family's teaching that dedicated, educated individuals could and should seek to improve their world. Thus, the emphasis her family placed on industriousness, education, patriotism, and even its ideal of the proper southern lady never left Blanton. She used these principles to propel herself to achievements that were extensive and rare for a woman then, while at the same time she continued to respect the traditions they represented. By entering the socially acceptable (and predominantly female) field of teaching and, subsequently, pushing to new limits as a woman reformer within this profession, Blanton created a successful blend of progress and tradition that proved a hallmark of her career. Years after her own career had been established, just as Texas women were about to achieve the right to vote in primaries, she wrote to Texas suffrage leader Minnie Fisher Cunningham and explained how Progressive-era reform efforts were analogous to the efforts of Blanton's ancestors who had fought for Texas independence: "I think that your name ought to be placed with those of other Texas heroes. You have fought as great a battle for freedom as they did, and, as the descendant of one of them, I am proud to be able to say this of a Texas woman."[10]

In 1867, Blanton's parents, Thomas Lindsay and Eugenia Webb Blanton, met and married in LaGrange, Texas. Her father, a native of Prince Edward County, Virginia, and a descendant of Capt. William Walker, who participated in the American Revolution, had ridden with the Confederate cavalry in Texas. He moved to Houston with his mother as a young boy, and after the Civil War he lived in LaGrange, where he met Eugenia Webb, whose forebears had settled in Fayette County in 1839.[11]

Annie Webb Blanton's maternal ancestors achieved a certain notoriety in Texas history. Her mother's grandfather, Asa Hill, received a land grant and moved his family to Texas from Georgia in the 1830s. Once they had arrived, Asa and his sons became active participants in the area's struggle for independence from Mexico. After the Texas Revolution, the family settled in Fayette County, and later, in 1842, the father and sons joined Texas forces attempting to drive Mexicans from the town of Mier. When the Texans were captured, Asa Hill's young son, John, impressed Mexican commanders Pedro Ampudia and Antonio López de Santa Anna with his bravery. Though imprisoned at Perote, Asa and another son survived; they had avoided drawing the black beans in a lottery, which designated who would be executed, and eventually they returned home safely in 1844. John, however, spent most of the rest of his life in Mexico, where he became a road engineer. To many, his bravery in the face of capture always made him the "boy hero of the Mier Expedition," a legacy in which his descendants, including Blanton and her immediate family, took great pride.[12]

Asa and his wife, Elizabeth Barksdale Hill, brought to Texas a family of twelve children. In 1848 their eleventh child, Sarah Ann Amelia, married William Graham Webb, a man who shared the Hill family's commitment to patriotism. Born in Georgia in 1824, he came to Texas in 1844, gained admittance to the bar in LaGrange in 1845, served with the United States during the Mexican War, and represented Fayette County in the Texas House of Representatives in 1847 and 1848. A staunch supporter of the Confederacy, he joined men considerably younger than himself in the 22nd Brigade of the Texas Militia in the Civil War. Afterward he assisted in the planning of the University of Texas and became proprietor of the Democratic *Daily Houston Telegraph*.[13] Webb was sympathetic with the concerns of Texans who resented Republican interference in their government and schools. Just a few weeks before his granddaughter, Annie Webb, was born, he wrote in the issue of his paper for July 29, 1870, that Texas faced a Herculean task in redeeming itself "from the control of the most hungry set of Radical vultures that ever preyed upon the liberties of a free people."[14]

Webb's newspaper work caused the family to live temporarily in Houston, but they all considered LaGrange their home. The Webb's eldest child, Annie Webb Blanton's mother Eugenia, was born in LaGrange in 1849, and it was there that, in 1867, she married Thomas Lindsay Blanton before moving to Houston with him.[15] Located one hundred miles east of LaGrange, Houston was the nearest large city, and as many young couples late in the nineteenth century had done, the newlywed Blantons went in search of opportunities in the burgeoning trade town. Although frontier roughness still characterized Houston in many ways, the majority of its population in 1870 was native to the South, and cultural activities and educational facilities were readily available. Because of relevant changes in the state constitution after the Civil War, this city of approximately ten thousand residents experienced much growth in the banking industry during the 1860s and 1870s, and in 1867 Thomas Blanton secured a job there as a bank teller. It was in Houston that Eugenia bore seven children in their home: May (July 2, 1868), Fannie Ligon and Annie Webb (August 19, 1870), Thomas Lindsay (October 25, 1872), Faerie (July 11, 1874), William Walker (October 11, 1876), and Eugene (July 28, 1879).[16]

Eugenia Webb and Thomas Blanton were both descended from families that emphasized one's personal duty to contribute to society, and they believed that education, even more than religion, was the central foundation for such contributions. Their affiliation with the Methodist church resulted in an abiding, but mostly private, Christian faith within the family. Their emphasis on education, however, was more evident. The Blantons were not financially wealthy, but they were determined to see that their children were provided proper, albeit not elaborate, schooling. In the 1870s, when Annie Webb Blanton began her formal education, the Reconstruction battles over a state school system had not yet been resolved, and attendance at private schools was common. Thus Blanton's initial enrollment (and probably that of her

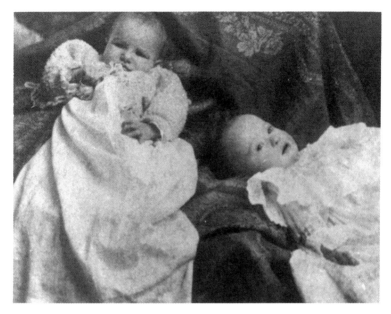

Twins Annie (*left*) and Fannie Blanton. (Photo courtesy The Delta Kappa Gamma Society International, copyright 1970.)

siblings) in a private school in Houston indicated more about the Texas educational system in the 1870s than that the family was seeking an elite education for its children. Houston did not institute a free public school system until 1877, and this program, racially and ethnically segregated, was only for children aged eight to fourteen years. As Blanton grew older, however, her parents did move her into the public school system and planned for her to graduate from Houston High School.[17]

A series of family tragedies altered these plans by changing familial commitments for the Blanton children, especially the daughters. On July 29, 1879, the day after the Blantons' son Eugene was born, thirty-year-old Eugenia died from childbirth complications. Left alone with seven children, the eldest of whom was eleven, Thomas moved his family back to LaGrange, where his own mother lived. She came to play a major role in raising the Blanton children, but during the years in LaGrange, the three oldest daughters, May, Annie, and Fannie, matured quickly as they assumed surrogate mother roles for their younger siblings. Annie's interest lay particularly in reading to the children and creating stories to entertain them, habits she later enjoyed sharing with nieces and nephews. She continued her own education in the LaGrange schools, but her responsibilities to her family increased in 1885, when her twin sister Fannie was stricken with a childhood disease and died. The Blanton children were close and the loss was difficult, especially for Annie, who shared a special affection for her twin. Shocked that Fannie, who generally had been more healthy than she, had died, Annie relied on her older sister May as a source of strength during this time.[18]

Although little remains in the historical record to help explain exactly what motivated Blanton to continue her education, by the time she graduated from LaGrange High School in 1887, she had determined to enter the University of Texas. There is no indication that she had been especially close to any college-educated women or that she had had any specific encouragement to attend college. Yet, her determination was real, and it persisted, even though family matters necessitated a temporary postponement. When her sister May married Frank Webb Hill (a cousin) and moved to Austin, Annie saw her immediate priority as continuing to help her younger siblings while simultaneously establishing her own financial independence in order to ease her father's responsibilities. By then, almost seventeen and with a high school diploma, she understood that a teaching job offered in a rural Fayette County town would enable her to be on her own monetarily without taking her too far from her family. Standards for rural education were far from stringent in 1887, and the one-room, one-teacher school in Pine Springs welcomed the bright, hard-working teenager.[19]

Located approximately eighteen miles southwest of LaGrange, Pine Springs was a small, agrarian community. Blanton boarded in a farm home nearby, and, although she was determined to succeed, she found the separation from her family difficult. Her brother Thomas, who made the initial horse-and-buggy drive to Pine Springs with her, tried to persuade her to forsake her new job and to return home with him, but she was resolved both to help her family and to launch her career. Probably because she had previously assumed important family responsibilities and already looked ahead to attend college, young Blanton took on this task with a sense of seriousness and dedication.[20]

To enter the teaching profession as Blanton did was by no means an unusual experience for young, middle-class females at this time. In the mid-nineteenth century, women gradually began to replace men as teachers, both for financial and pedagogical reasons. Advocates of teaching as women's "true" profession, such as Catharine Beecher, believed that women were well-suited to the classroom because of their special nurturing skills and their ability to set a moral tone in communities. They also argued that teaching provided a respectable alternative to marriage, as well as some sense of independence for women without threatening the proper boundaries of "femininity." Beecher's vision became dominant for a variety of reasons. Economically, schools could pay women less because it was understood that they worked temporarily, only until they married, and because they had no family to support. Demographically, the growing population in the United States, coupled with the movement of increasing numbers of males into industrial and commercial work, opened teaching positions for women. From 1840 to 1880, more and more educators were female, and society even began to perceive teaching as a woman-oriented profession. This perception continued after the Civil War, and by the end of the 1880s, 63 percent of American teachers were women; in cities, women constituted 90 percent of the teaching force at that time.[21] In 1881, a guidebook for wage-earning women noted that teaching had long been popular as employment for the educated "principally because it [provided] one of the few means of money-making in which a lady may openly engage without compromising her social standing." Another, later observation on teaching as appropriate work for women noted that, compared with most occupations, teaching was "genteel, paid reasonably well, and required little special skill or equipment." Thus, accepting the job at Pine Springs would have seemed a logical and even traditional decision for a woman of Blanton's background. Blanton's determination to move on from this job, to receive her college degree, and to pursue a career —all in place of marriage—was less common.[22]

Blanton did not often, in later years, refer specifically to her teaching experiences in Pine Springs; nevertheless, the one-year session clearly influenced her ideas concerning the needs of rural schools. Following her election in 1918 as state superintendent of public instruction for Texas, she made rural school education a priority for her administration, and later, as a professor at the University of Texas, she was instrumental in the formation of a rural education division within the university's school of education. She wished there, she said, "to champion the cause of the children at the forks of the creek, who for two generations have been discriminated against in Texas education."[23] Blanton believed that her firsthand experience in rural Pine Springs had given her a lifelong, unique insight into the persistent problems in this area of education. In an effort to convey this experience to her students, she required visits to rural schools as part of the university classes she taught on the subject.[24] In her race for the U.S. Congress in 1922, she also made a strong appeal to farmers and other rural voters, indicating her readiness to represent these constituents.[25]

Pine Springs, then, provided important professional experience for Blanton, but she had never intended to make her life's career there. Proposals to marry came from some of her students, who were very near her own age, but were declined, as she still planned to enroll in the university as soon as she felt she could leave her family and manage her own finances.

After a year in Pine Springs, however, a family matter once again affected her plans. Her father's death in 1888 left Blanton's family in a state of disarray. Financial matters were, of course, worsened for Blanton's siblings, and the third family death in less than ten years drew the Blanton children even closer. Despite the difficulties of uprooting the family, an immediate move to Austin increasingly appealed to Blanton because it would reunite the family with their older sister May and their maternal grandfather, William Webb, who had recently moved there. In addition, such a move would place Annie near the university, provide better teaching opportunities, and offer increased job possibilities for the children as they reached working age. Therefore, joined by their paternal grandmother, Blanton and her four younger siblings moved to the capital city soon after their father's death.[26]

Although the move to Austin had probably come about sooner than she had originally expected, Blanton readily made the most of the opportunity to live in the town where she could proceed with her college goals. First, she took the qualifying examination for a teaching position in the Austin city schools and was subsequently hired to teach at East Austin Elementary (and later at West Austin). Then, in 1892, after several years of simultaneously maintaining her teaching duties and financially and emotionally supporting her younger siblings, Blanton enrolled as an undergraduate student at the University of Texas.[27]

The university had opened in Austin in 1883, some fifty years after discussions had begun in the Republic of Texas concerning such an institution of higher education. The new school, endowed by land in West Texas, had been designed to offer educational opportunities to as many white citizens of the state as possible. Coeducational from its founding, it represented the less-elite approach to higher education that was spreading across the country during the latter part of the nineteenth century. Although the all-male Agricultural and Mechanical College had opened in Bryan in 1876, most other institutions of higher education in Texas in the 1880s were privately financed or primarily preparatory in nature. Thus, given her situation and choices, the University of Texas was easily the most logical place for a young woman such as Annie Webb Blanton to enroll. It offered a reputable degree, was near her sister, and was as affordable as any other higher education facility. It welcomed women and was located in a town large enough to offer her gainful employment while she pursued her work there.[28]

Even with a teaching job, Blanton faced the difficult financial burden of paying university tuition at the same time that she helped to support her family. Consequently, her enrollment was irregular, consisting primarily of summer and evening classes, which she took as frequently as time and money permitted. In her studies, she concentrated on English, education, and French, and, in 1899, after seven years of work and at the age of twenty-nine, she finally was awarded the Bachelor of Literature degree.

The degree brought a salary increase to sixty-six dollars a month for her last year at Pease Elementary and a promotion to a position as an English teacher at Austin High for the 1900–1901 school year. [29]

Having now achieved her dream of a college education, Blanton soon left Austin to pursue even more ambitious career goals. Her years in Austin had proven her ability to patiently carry out multiple tasks and to demand much of herself, traits that would mark the rest of her career as an educator. Though she had sacrificed some extracurricular activities in order to achieve her goal, she did not dwell upon her difficulties; her determination replaced any regrets. Later, as a faculty member at the University of Texas, Blanton summarized her student years in a typically resolute manner: "As I taught during the time of my undergraduate work, I had no leisure for participation in social activities."[30]

Blanton never expressed any bitterness that her brother Thomas, who was two years her junior and a future United States congressman, had had a somewhat easier tenure at the university. With the money he had saved from his job at an Austin grocery store, Thomas entered the university the same year as his sister, but, by 1897, two years before Annie graduated, he had received both an academic and a law degree. He also had found time to win a university tennis championship, play football, and participate as a debater. [31] The collegiate experiences of brother and sister illustrate the different expectations which society and family held for males and females, but, in this specific case, there arose no resentment. Blanton was proud of her brother, and his university experience in no way distracted her from her own goals. She entered the twentieth century with her own college degree, as well as teaching experience in rural and city schools at both elementary and secondary levels. Considering the personal family misfortunes she had experienced and the social barriers that then existed for women who pursued college degrees, the serious-minded Blanton knew she had accomplished a major feat and had no reason to perceive her experience as in any way deficient.

Blanton's first thirty years established important patterns for her life. Her abiding closeness and loyalty to family members, forged from the series of family deaths, and her engrained pride in her ancestors never wavered. From these ancestors she had inherited a strong sense of patriotism, as well as a commitment to the betterment of society. Blanton's devotion to education as a career probably arose from her family's belief in the importance of preparing future generations to be responsible citizens, just as their own pioneer parents had taught them.[32] Her heritage was steeped in southern values: she attended racially segregated schools, was taught the evils of overt interference by the federal government, and was raised to value independence. She also learned and practiced the domestic skills of a southern lady, fulfilling many maternal duties after her mother's death. Together, these elements had created a heavy emphasis on tradition and the idea of upholding expected roles; Blanton never sought to avoid this inheritance or completely to break from it. Later in her career, while actively involved in solving school problems that had resulted largely from nineteenth-century southern reaction against outside influence — a stance shared by many in her own family — Blanton never considered her efforts to be in conflict with her heritage. In her attempts to improve Texas schools, she may have moved beyond her family's concern about the influence of the Republican Party in the South, but she never departed from their ties to the Democratic Party or the notion that good citizens were obligated to contribute to society. While serving as state superintendent, she once noted that she was a member of the Democratic Party because she believed it favored the rights of the people and because she, as a loyal southerner, continued to cherish the best ideals of the Old South.[33]

Indeed, Blanton's reform efforts consistently reflected a racial bias and prejudice against any serious weakening of states' rights. As did many southern Progressives, she desired to preserve the cultural values of her region while reforming specific aspects of it. She joined these reformers in recognizing that education was a vehicle for developing an improved South. Concerns for blacks and black education were not prominent in that framework. Her career choice of teaching also reflected a socially acceptable, traditional profession for single women at the end of the nineteenth century.

Still, before 1900, she had already shown a determination that would distinguish her from other teachers. Blanton refused to see a career in education as a dead end with no opportunity for professional advancement.[34] She had a strong desire to become well-educated and well-trained and to use her professional experiences in order to pursue a worthwhile career that provided both self-satisfaction and a sense of social contribution. Family responsibilities, financial difficulties, and full schedules—Blanton accepted these as challenges rather than hindrances, and by 1901 she was ready, literally and figuratively, to move on. Although she had yet to articulate a clear call for progressive reform for either schools or women, Blanton had firmly established her sense of personal ambition and ability. These characteristics, influenced but not limited by the traditional values of her family, took her to the North Texas town of Denton, where her career as an educational leader and reformer began.

Denton

1 9 0 1 - 1 8

A nervous normal-school teacher stood before her colleagues at the 1916 meeting of the Texas State Teachers Association in Fort Worth and asked, quietly but firmly, that the membership give some thought to broadening the role of women in the organization. Even though Blanton was a classroom teacher, she did not enjoy addressing large groups and this was not a particularly easy speech for her to make. But since 1887, when she had taken the job at Pine Springs, she had increasingly seen the barriers placed in front of women educators — regardless of their capabilities. By 1916, her experiences at North Texas State Normal College in Denton had not only confirmed those impressions but also allowed her to develop a close comradeship with other female teachers, who both shared her views and experiences and helped to shape her ideas. She felt obliged to try to correct the inequities inflicted upon her and her female colleagues and to try to attain greater opportunities for professional contributions by capable women teachers. Thus, she turned to the most visible and important teachers' group in the state to articulate her ideas. When she left the meeting of that group in 1916, no longer was Annie Webb Blanton merely a normal-school teacher — she was president-elect of the Texas State Teachers Association. As the first woman to attain that position, she not only had proven her effectiveness in persuading others of her own ideas but had also ensured that her own anonymity as a schoolteacher had ended.

The broadening of American higher education in the late nineteenth century included the development and expansion of normal schools devoted to training those students who planned to become teachers. By the beginning of the twentieth century these institutions, combined with the rising number of state universities and land grant colleges, offered increased opportunities for students who wished to attend college and created a larger pool of faculty positions for aspiring professors.[1] Blanton's graduation from the University of Texas conveniently coincided with the rise of normal schools in the state.

In 1900, Texas had only one state school for training white teachers, Sam Houston Normal Institute at Huntsville, which had opened in 1879, and one institution for training black teachers, which had been established at the same time in Prairie View.[2] By 1920, the state had created six additional white teacher training schools — in Denton (1901), San Marcos (1903), Canyon (1910), Commerce (1917), Nacogdoches (1918), and Alpine (1919). The rapid establishment of these institutions reflected both the belief of many early twentieth-century Texans that the development of an improved public school system would have to include well-trained teachers and the acknowledgment that, in a state so geographically large, several institutions would be needed to accomplish this goal. Despite the lofty ideals that undergirded their establishment and their increased numbers, the schools were not immediately able to provide a competitive higher education curriculum. Nor were they the only institutions that offered teacher training. The state accredited numerous other denominational, independent, state, and municipal colleges to teach courses leading to certification. New normal schools struggled against this preexisting competition, as well as to keep their own standards high enough to meet accreditation regulations and provide course work that emphasized pedagogical skills yet offered college-level challenges. Most normal schools consequently found it necessary to raise their standards progressively after first having operated at precollege (or high school) levels. State education leaders thought, however, that the potential of normal schools was worth the problems they initially posed because, unlike those schools which happened to be approved for teacher certification in addition to their other offerings, normals had been created to train teachers exclusively, and they thus offered the potential for state standardization of such training.[3]

In 1901, the state based its selection of Denton as the site for a new normal institution on the rapidly increasing population in the North Texas region and the existence of a private normal in the town since 1890.[4] In that year, Joshua Crittenden Chilton, a Michigan educator and strong advocate of coeducation, had arrived in Denton and opened his private, independent Texas Normal College. Denton's civic leaders had initially encouraged the privately funded school and had constructed a three-story brick building to house it. By the late 1890s, however, the municipal powers perceived that, despite some success, the school posed too great a financial burden for the city. Nonetheless the private school did alert local leaders to Denton's potential as a site for a new state-funded school with similar goals in the North Texas area. After several attempts, in 1899, Denton politicians succeeded in persuading the state legislature to pass a bill creating North Texas State Normal College; the new school received state funding in 1901 and opened in August of that year, absorbing what had remained of Chilton's institution.[5]

Texas usually placed its normal schools in small, conservative towns that had some potential for growth yet were conducive to providing a proper atmosphere for future teachers. When Blanton moved to Denton in 1901, the town had just over four thousand residents, although during the seventeen years that she lived there it grew to almost double that size. Created in 1856 as a new, central location for the Denton County seat, the town had prospered steadily until 1890, when it entered a decade of municipal, educational, and cultural growth. The founding of the private normal college and the establishment of railroad connections to Dallas and Fort Worth were important to Denton's growth, as were the arrival of streetcars, a brick plant, a new courthouse and jail, a new opera house, and the founding of several women's clubs. The city's permanent participation in higher education efforts was solidified early in the twentieth century with the state's involvement in the normal school and with the establishment of the Girls Industrial College (later the College of Industrial Arts, and now Texas Woman's University) in 1902. Denton demonstrated its commitment to keep such educational facilities by vot-

ing in 1902 to prohibit the manufacture and sale of liquor anywhere within Denton County. The town was proud of its whole-
some atmosphere, and North Texas State Normal College reflected this environment with its emphasis on discipline and
professional preparation.[6]

The new state normal attracted students primarily from nearby
farms and small towns—white Protestant sons and daughters of
farmers, ranchers, and merchants. Their average age was twenty,
and in the early years of the school, most of them did not have
high school degrees. In its early history, the facility identified
its mandate and objectives this way:

> The Normal is neither a college nor a university. The statute cre-
> ating the institution declares its purpose to be "for the special
> training of teachers," and any marked deviation from the course
> . . . would be a violation of legislative intent as expressed in this
> law. Accordingly, in its course of study the school must hold in
> view the needs of the twelve thousand white teachers required
> annually for the public schools of Texas. Using the public school
> branches as a basis, it must deal with and seek to develop these
> fundamental principles which underlie all education. Therefore,
> the Normal has its own sphere of work apart from the high school
> and academy on the one hand and the college and university on
> the other.[7]

A major advantage North Texas had in hiring its initial faculty members was the recruitment of Joel Sutton Kendall as the
school's first president. Kendall, an educator who had risen from
rural Texas teaching to become state superintendent of public
instruction in 1900, lent immediate credibility to the new school
in Denton. Both Kendall and his successor, William Herschel
Bruce, provided for Blanton examples of teachers who, like herself, had started their careers in small rural schools and subsequently had joined the highest ranks of education in Texas.

Even with Kendall as president, the faculty, facilities, and curriculum at North Texas in 1901 were hardly representative of the
kind of higher education Blanton had experienced as a student—
and would again later as a faculty member—at the University
of Texas. Nevertheless, the teaching opportunities afforded by
the Denton facility were slightly better than what would have

been found at a high school, and Blanton saw in the normal school the challenge of a new position. By applying to North Texas, Blanton reaffirmed her serious commitment to a career as a professional educator. She took the position with a realistic understanding of the limited role of normal schools but recognized it as an opportunity to move to a higher level of teaching. And, because her youngest sibling Eugene was now twenty-two years old, Blanton felt comfortable with her decision to leave Austin and her family to move more than two hundred miles north to Denton.[8]

Blanton's new colleagues were mostly instructors, like herself, with no teaching experience beyond the elementary or secondary school level. With annual salaries ranging only from around eleven hundred dollars (for the least-experienced females) to two thousand dollars (for the president), the school, like most normal schools, simply could not demand more experienced faculty. The training and backgrounds of the fourteen individuals who comprised North Texas' first faculty were more varied than their experience levels: several had no college degree, three held both bachelor's and master's degrees, one was a graduate of Yale, and several others were normal school graduates. Only one faculty member remained from the earlier private normal school.[9] Blanton was the only University of Texas undergraduate alumna. Eight of the fourteen faculty members were women; only one of this group held an advanced degree. In general, normal schools included more women on their faculties than other colleges and universities; often, as the newest and least-established college-level institutions, they provided an entry for female faculty members that more traditional institutions denied. The gender ratio at North Texas (about 57 percent) coincided closely with the national average (63.4 percent) at public normal schools in 1900.[10]

Although Blanton's new position was in a small town, her new home did not lack cultural and educational outlets. And even if North Texas was limited in its course offerings, it still provided an opportunity for career advancement that appealed to her. The woman who left Denton in 1918 had noticeably matured as an educator and political leader from the thirty-one-year-old secondary teacher who had arrived there in 1901. During that time she had also developed a close circle of women friends, who would influence her personal and professional choices throughout her life.

Despite their increasing numerical strength in institutions of higher education, women professors often found themselves in the lowest ranking jobs at the lowest salaries, and they were usually denied mentor relationships with senior male faculty members. Such difficulties elicited various reactions from female professors. Some chose to become closer to one another and pursue a united effort to abolish age-old gender prejudices. Others decided that academic success required only objective and rational devotion to their specific areas of study; these women emphasized professional competence over gender unity.[11] Blanton combined these approaches, becoming a champion of gender unity as a means to affect change, while at the same time insisting that women prove their competence before being afforded equality. Blanton used this philosophy to maintain generally cooperative relationships with her male colleagues, a characteristic which would become a key element to her future successes.

Joining the small faculty at North Texas presented Blanton with opportunities for friendship, professional role models, and joint extracurricular activities. From male faculty members, she learned the value of participating in statewide professional teaching endeavors. As a former state superintendent, President Kendall was an experienced educational leader, and his successor in 1906, Dr. Bruce, was a leader in the Texas State Teachers Association. Although neither became a true personal mentor to Blanton—later she tangled with Bruce over both educational and political matters—she nevertheless broadened her professionalism by learning from them. Later, during her tenures in both the teachers' association presidency and the office of state superintendent, she drew upon the experience of having worked for veterans of these offices.[12]

Blanton's relationships with female faculty members proved more multifaceted. Early in her tenure at North Texas, she joined with Annie Moore, an instructor in primary methods, to assist female students in forming the Current Literature Club. She also joined female faculty members in participating in and leading the local Woman's Shakespeare Club and City Federation of

Women's Clubs. These activities indicate Blanton's choice, from this point in her life onward, to devote her personal endeavors to those concerns associated primarily with women. Blanton's living arrangements in Denton reflected her woman-centered world. Upon moving to North Texas, Blanton lived briefly in a boarding home before renting a house on a cooperative basis with other female teachers. Eventually she borrowed money to build her own four-bedroom home on West Mulberry Street in Denton, and here she invited a few women teachers to live with her. Located closer to downtown and farther from the campus than most faculty homes, Blanton's abode was well-known in Denton for its weekly Sunday evening buffets for teachers and friends and for its large rose garden, cared for by all who shared the home. The women ate at a boarding house during the week, but Blanton, who considered herself an accomplished cook, used the kitchen in her home for entertaining and allowed the women to enjoy themselves there at their leisure on the weekends. Comfortable domesticity was important to Blanton and her friends, and their home was designed to offer them this element without requiring too much time from their busy professional schedules.[13] Within this context, Blanton was able to express her femininity freely.

Blanton formed many friendships with her female colleagues, including a very close one with Emma Mitchell. A native of Paris, Texas, Mitchell had studied Latin and history at the University of Chicago before returning to Paris to teach in elementary and secondary schools. In 1901 she joined the first faculty of North Texas as an instructor in history and soon became friends with Blanton. Sharing a desire to travel and to learn more of the world, the two toured Europe together in the summer of 1907. Mitchell assisted Blanton during her presidency of the state teachers' association in 1917 and advised Blanton when she considered leaving North Texas in 1918. That same year, when Blanton was elected state superintendent, Mitchell resigned her teaching position to become second assistant state superintendent and later director of the State Board of Examiners in Blanton's administration. Upon moving to Austin in 1918, Blanton and Mitchell shared a room in a friend's home and took their meals together at the university faculty club.[14] The two women remained close over the years in Austin, although their living arrangements eventually changed. Throughout her life Blanton maintained close relationships with a few favorite friends, including, for many years, Mitchell.[15] Such friendships marked the beginning of Blanton's lifelong reliance on women for both personal and professional support, friendship, and long-term commitments. Blanton found the company of women—in both individual and group relationships—enjoyable, comfortable, and rewarding. At the professional level, this preference manifested itself over the next thirty years in her work to achieve equality for women teachers through the Texas State Teachers Association, the State Department of Education, Delta Kappa Gamma, and numerous other professional women's associations. On a personal level, it reflected her decision to remain single and to avoid romantic involvement with men. Relationships with Mitchell and others were intimate and took the place of marriage in Blanton's life, supplying her with support, motivation, and strength. Blanton was clearly committed to other women in both practical and emotional terms. Her personal arrangements with other women, though not brief, appear less permanent and exclusive than the longstanding commitment involved in the "Boston marriage" unions that some female couples entered into; still, in her own way, she made women the focus of both her personal and professional life, and her interaction with them played a more central than incidental part in the success of her feminist efforts.[16]

Just as Denton had provided the background for Blanton to make important decisions regarding her personal environment, it also proved a place of professional maturation for her. Hired by North Texas to teach English grammar and composition, she held the rank of associate professor for her seventeen years in Denton, carrying the standard semester teaching load of five classes meeting five times a week and filling additional administrative duties as expected.[17] A woman with a high energy level, she thrived on her rigorous teaching schedule and threw herself into numerous other school activities, usually of a nature that kept her in direct contact with students. In addition to her work with the women's Current Literature Club, which provided a dominant social and intellectual activity for students at North Texas, she also coached the debate team and established the *North Texas State Normal Journal* for students to develop their publication skills. Though at times her rigorous schedule left her physically worn, she indicated no resentment at the demands of her career as an educator.[18]

Blanton enjoyed her students and identified with them. The typical North Texas pupil was the child of a rural environment — preparing, often at some financial difficulty, to teach school and residing away from home, usually for the first time, in one of Denton's ubiquitous boardinghouses. Blanton showed sympathy to the hardships such individuals encountered, and she took personal interest in them, although never lowering her expectations or becoming a "soft touch" in the process. In 1908, the school yearbook, *The Yucca,* was dedicated to her in "respectful tribute to her justice, impartiality, and interest in the students."[19]

Because Blanton specialized in English grammar, she found herself routinely assigned to administer the school's grammar examination to incoming students. This experience made her aware of vast deficiencies in the students' preparation, a fact she found troubling and inappropriate for future teachers. At one point she complained to President Bruce that it seemed absurd to graduate future teachers of high school English who lacked the ability to construct ordinary sentences.[20] Blanton recognized that one problem in the teaching of grammar was the lack of good textbooks, both for training teachers and for teachers to use in secondary classrooms. Although her schedule and workload were quite full and normal school faculty rarely published books, the energetic Blanton determined to prepare several small grammar books herself. By 1910, she had written two texts, both published by the Charles E. Merrill Company of New York: *Review Outline and Exercises in English Grammar* and *Supplemental Exercises in Punctuation and Composition.* The books soon spread beyond North Texas, as many public school districts across the country, including 150 cities in New York, adopted them.[21] These publication efforts distinguished Blanton from most of her colleagues and provided her some name recognition with educators outside Denton. Her career as a professor was further enhanced by graduate work, including grammar studies, undertaken at the University of Chicago during the summers of 1901, 1913, and 1914, as well as at the University of Texas in 1910.[22] With the publication of her books, her ambitious pursuit to further her own education, and her increasing involvement in professional teacher organizations, Blanton laid the foundation for a more prominent role for herself in Texas education.

Early in her career at North Texas, Blanton became an enthusiastic joiner, eager to be an active member of numerous organizations. This desire sprang from the general sense of civic responsibility she had inherited from her family, as well as from a conviction that such involvement put one in contact with those with similar interests, and, possibly, those who could be of professional assistance. While in Denton her memberships included the local and state Federation of Women's Clubs, the Daughters of the Confederacy, the Texas Parent-Teachers' Association, and the Eastern Star.[23] One of her strongest commitments, however, was to the Texas State Teachers Association (TSTA). President Bruce, as a former president of TSTA, encouraged his teachers to participate in this important organization. By 1912, Blanton was an active member of the association, attending every annual meeting, becoming familiar with the politics of the group, and encouraging other teachers, especially women, at North Texas and elsewhere to join.[24]

Blanton's participation in TSTA was closely related to her growing concern about women's roles in the teaching profession. As her own career as an educator and author prospered in the 1910s, Blanton's awareness of the professional discrimination that women encountered as a result of their gender continued to grow. This awareness, no doubt reinforced by her network of close female friends at North Texas, grew simultaneously with the burgeoning suffrage movement in Texas. Yet, she did not limit her goals to obtaining voting rights for women. Blanton believed that her female colleagues experienced a broader gamut of problems of inequality that needed prompt attention—from salary inequities to unfair representation in teachers' groups to underutilization as talented professionals.

Central to what she saw as the answer to these problems was

the idea that women could better work together as a united force to address their grievances than as individuals seeking isolated improvements primarily of benefit to themselves. Her desires for women teachers encompassed three principles: women should strive for excellence, women who had proven their professional competence should not be denied opportunities merely on account of their gender, and professional women should never forsake their womanhood but rather use it to enhance their work and home. Despite their unselfish motivation, these goals—which reflect the very essence of Blanton's feminism—remained largely class and race specific; she did not seek to broaden the pool of women teachers but rather to improve opportunities specifically for competent, middle-class, white women in the profession. She had no use for those women she considered inept or lazy, nor was she actively concerned with the plight of black teachers or lower-class women, but she firmly believed that proven women of her own race and class deserved the same opportunities as men of this group. Through the forum of the state teachers' association, Blanton enunciated her ideas as well as built her statewide reputation as an educator.[25]

For Blanton, the TSTA initially presented an ironic dualism. The organization provided rewarding professional comradery and the opportunity to stay informed about issues important to teachers. At the same time, however, the association was clearly hesitant to change its male-dominated leadership tradition, which stood in direct opposition to Blanton's ideals for women teachers. Created in 1880 in the Central Texas town of Mexia, the association was founded to coordinate the concerns and interests of white Texas schoolteachers and administrators from elementary through college levels. In 1885, black teachers, excluded from TSTA, formed the Colored Teachers State Association of Texas and worked through that organization until membership in TSTA was opened to them in 1963. During its early years, TSTA's resources and power were limited, but gradually it grew into an important organization in which professional educators could become acquainted with one another, listen to prominent speakers, and keep abreast of important issues in both the educational and political arenas. Though most teachers in Texas were not members, the most prominent ones were, and the organization took the lead in educational concerns and was closely watched by many Texas educators. Membership was open to women, and by the 1910s even some offices and committee posts had been given to them. But male leaders resisted the idea of electing a woman to the group's highest office. Consequently, and as the suffrage movement gained momentum, some women educators determined to nominate a woman for president at each annual convention. They recognized that it was unrealistic to expect victory, but they desired to make the point in principle that women were qualified and, accordingly, that they should be considered for this office.[26]

Blanton understood such tactics and sympathized with those opposed to the unfair barriers the organization used to keep women in subordinate roles. She believed, however, that most women recognized that the simple election of a female president would not necessarily improve their status as members and educators or that placing a token name on the ballot each year would accomplish anything substantial. Just as Blanton believed that suffrage alone was not as important as how women then used their vote both to prove themselves and to build a foundation for future opportunities, so she regarded the TSTA presidency as only a first step. Its attainment would be of little help to women if they were not prepared then to work for broader goals.[27] By November, 1916, Blanton was confident of these ideas and convinced that the organization's strengths could be better maintained through comprehensively increasing the role of its women members. Desiring to share her thoughts on these matters, which she believed represented most female association members, she arrived at the group's annual meeting in Fort Worth prepared to state her concerns. During the meeting, nominations for president proceeded in what had been their usual fashion: three men were nominated by three other men, and one woman was nominated by another woman. It was then that Blanton rose to speak:

> I have come before you not to advocate the election of any one person, though personally my vote goes for Mr. [J. W.] Beatty [Denton school superintendent]. But the women of the Texas State

Teachers' Association feel that there are some facts that should be laid before the Association. We think it makes no difference at this particular time whether a man or a woman is elected at the head of this Association, but we do believe that it makes a difference as to whether our present method of apportioning honors and apportioning authority and apportioning power in the State Teachers' Association shall continue.[28]

Blanton then assured the men that women had no desire to array themselves against the males but simply to achieve fair representation: "We do not want the vice-presidency forever. How long are the functions of the women of the State Teachers' Association to be limited to paying a dollar to support its activities and to that of acting as audience and applause? You have asserted this afternoon that you believe in a fair representation of all people; then, in the future, give us a chance."[29]

Blanton later said that this speech was not formally prepared in advance, "but I had it in me, and when I rose to talk, it came out."[30] The words captivated her audience, whose male members appreciated an appeal based on common sense and reason rather than emotion or politics. Blanton apparently did not expect immediate results and was surprised when A. B. Sewell of Abilene then nominated her to become the association's president. She immediately objected to her nomination, citing her preference not to run against Denton candidate Beatty or against one of the other candidates who represented a normal school. It is noteworthy that she voiced no objection to running against the other female candidate, whose name had been placed in contention only as a token and eventually would be withdrawn by the nominator in favor of Blanton.[31] A woman member seconded Blanton's nomination, noting, "It needs no one to speak on behalf of Miss Blanton. Texas knows her; and I know we will all unite behind Miss Blanton."[32] Over her own objections, the association elected Blanton by a comfortable margin over the male candidates and, thus, she became the first woman president of TSTA in the organization's thirty-six year history.[33] The prominent *Texas School Journal* lauded her election, noting that she was a "woman who has attained high professional standing as a teacher and as a student of educational questions."[34]

For the rest of her life, Blanton maintained that her election had been a complete surprise and had represented no behind-the-scenes political maneuvering. Whether she truly had not anticipated election remains uncertain, but it is clear that her pre-convention activities had included collaboration with other female members to develop her ideas and to assess the desires of her female colleagues. This preparation, coupled with her directly worded presentation, made for a very successful speech, despite the fact that it neither addressed any school reform issues beyond the role of women nor advocated anything close to a working platform.[35]

The importance of Blanton's election and its effect on her future career cannot be overstated. Even though education was an accepted professional arena for women, her election to this leadership role extended the prescribed boundaries of women's role in the teaching profession. At its most personal level, the election indicated respect and admiration from her colleagues. For a man to be elected president, such a vote of confidence was an honor; for a woman it represented honor *and* unusual opportunity, a fact Blanton fully recognized. Soon after her election, she reflected on her situation: "I don't know how to express my appreciation of the honor. I had no idea of such a thing, of course. I am glad, not for any personal reason, but because it is the first recognition women ever have obtained in the association, and I think they are entitled to it."[36] Her election also offered proof that she could articulate her ideas well to a large crowd, no small feat for a woman who disdained public speeches and who, by her own admission and the testimony of colleagues and students, lacked the skills of a lively lecturer. Learning that she could perform successfully as a public speaker, even without enjoying it, was important for her and came to affect future decisions in her public career.[37]

The election also brought Blanton praise and publicity. The *Denton Record-Chronicle* lauded her precedent-breaking election, noting that it proved Denton's high ranking as an educational city.[38] As telegrams poured in from former University of Texas classmates, North Texas celebrated the event with a special chapel service featuring congratulatory speeches by faculty members and civic leaders as well as songs and yells from students.[39]

The election also reinforced Blanton's belief that she could work for increased opportunities for women without alienating men. After assuming office, she used the male support she had garnered in Fort Worth to keep a perspective on what the election truly represented in her own eyes: "The occasion [of election] is, perhaps, remarkable, not so much in that, for the first time, a woman fills this office, but in that for the first time it is held by a member of the rank and file of the teaching profession."[40] But in the same speech, she reminded male colleagues of women's ideals for the organization: "We plead guilty to the desire to have a voice in all of the affairs of this body. But there should be no question in this Association as to the domination of either sex, and no objection on the part of either, to the admission of the views of the other."[41] Thus, for Blanton, women offered the association skills and talents that complemented men's. She never advocated minimizing femininity or having female members attempt simply to imitate their male colleagues. Blanton believed that women could prove their equal abilities while maintaining their differences from men, and that both groups could work together harmoniously.

Blanton took office early in 1917, fulfilling her duties out of Denton so that she could retain her position at North Texas. She found the year to be challenging, and at times even exhausting.[42] Even though males had helped elect her, she nevertheless encountered resistance from some members, who had no desire to follow the lead of a female president. Thus, despite her efforts at harmony, the gender issue did not quietly fade away, and later Blanton recalled that, "while I had the friendly help of many good men, there was always a faction with narrow prejudices who opposed everything that I attempted, not because there was no merit in what I was seeking, but because of the fact that the one initiating it was a woman."[43]

Still, the faction did not keep her from remaining on good terms with most members or achieving several significant reforms as president. The role of women in education and in the association was a clear focus, although not a singular theme, of her efforts. Having assessed the poor monetary condition of the association, she planned and established a permanent fund to provide more secure financing. She also undertook and achieved constitutional revisions that she believed would afford a more democratic role for all TSTA members, particularly women. These revisions included allowing women to serve on the executive committee, holding members of this committee to only one successive term, allowing nominations for the committee from the convention floor, and making the president of the association the presiding officer of the committee. Blanton successfully introduced a resolution recommending the membership of women on school boards statewide and another establishing a permanent committee to work for a statewide teachers' retirement fund. The school board issue was backed by a nationwide survey she had compiled, which showed how prevalent and effective women board members were in other states. Women had served on school boards in Texas before Blanton's election, but some local areas attempted to bar women from their boards by requiring members to be qualified voters. Blanton's resolution aimed at ending this practice and also encouraging the election of women to the boards of institutions of higher education. In a move to end the frequent habit of electing the superintendent of the host city of the annual TSTA convention as president of the organization, she effectively led support for a constitutional change stating that no teacher who resided in the city of the annual meeting could be elected president that year.[44]

Blanton's year as president culminated with the annual convention held in Waco in November, 1917. She used this opportunity to bring exemplary women professionals before the association and to reinforce the goals she had worked for throughout the year. Featured speakers included Mary C. C. Bradford, state superintendent of Colorado and president of the National Education Association, and Ella Flagg Young, former superintendent of Chicago schools.[45] Perhaps showing a hint of plans she had for herself, Blanton wrote to fellow Texan Anna Pennybacker in reference to Bradford, "I want to show them what a woman state superintendent is like."[46] Blanton used the convention also to have male TSTA members show their support of her efforts, with San Antonio superintendent Charles S. Meek speaking on "Women as School Board Members" and *Texas School Journal* publisher H. T. Musselman addressing "Equal Pay for Equal Work."[47] Noting the preponderance of presentations on issues directly related to women, Blanton later wrote to Texas suffrage leader Minnie Fisher Cunningham, "The meeting of our State Teachers' Association was almost like a suffrage meeting."[48]

For her own presidential address Blanton chose to speak on "Democracy and the State Teachers' Association," using the 1917 wartime theme of worldwide democracy to reiterate her belief that the association had a responsibility to operate democratically. "Just now democracy is the watch-word of the world. The State Teachers' Association is the only potential citadel of democracy in the teaching profession in Texas," she told the group. Rather than portraying herself as similar to her male predecessors, Blanton emphasized her female perspective and offered comparisons only with others of her own sex. By directly confronting her experiences as the first woman president of TSTA, she clearly advocated a continued role of prominence for other talented women teachers. As she said:

> From early childhood, I have felt an intense sympathy for Eve. If she had realized that, for ages, her failings would be cited as a reproach to the rest of womankind, what a crushing sense of responsibility she must have experienced in that awful thought! The same feeling, in some degree, weighs upon the mind of any woman who is the first of her sex in any position of responsibility, however relatively unimportant it may be to that of mother Eve. She suffers the dread lest, through her ignorance, inexperience, or errors of judgment, some reflection shall be cast upon others of her sex. As the first woman in the office of president of the State Teachers' Association, I ask you to believe that, wherever I have failed in the duties of the present year, or may merit your disapproval in my words or actions at this convention, there are many other women of our profession in this State who would not thus have fallen short of your ideal.

Despite the modesty that Blanton projected in these words, she carefully made the point that other competent women needed to be afforded similar leadership opportunities in the future.[49]

There is no doubt that in a group with three thousand members there were those who did not support Blanton, and her election certainly did not end all sexist sentiment in the association. But for the most part, her presidency was a success, and her efforts were appreciated. Calling again upon her enormous energy, Blanton attended to small details of the organization while pursuing the larger goals that she believed would better TSTA—and, thus, the teaching profession in Texas. That she achieved many of her goals without alienating the majority of male members was significant for the continued improvement of women's opportunities. Because of her credentials as an educator and her leadership strengths as TSTA president, many of her male colleagues respected Blanton and appreciated her ability to pursue the issues of democracy and equality in ways that did not threaten them or the association. In her trademark way, Blanton advocated and worked for substantial changes without appearing radical or polemical.[50]

This ability was recognized both during and after her presidency. At the 1917 Waco meeting, a special resolution presented by J. P. Sewell, W. S. Sutton, and C. E. Evans praised Blanton's leadership skills. Many years later, a former student of Blanton's at the University of Texas noted that despite her unwavering efforts to achieve professional equality for women, many people who knew Blanton found it difficult to think of her as a strident idealogue for women's rights. Rather, it was her outstanding capabilities that people, including many men, remembered.[51]

Although some males refused to support her, and even though a man succeeded her, Blanton's election ended male dominance of the organization's highest office, opening the way for women to win increased leadership roles in TSTA. Blanton's immediate successor was William Bennett Bizzell, but in 1921 Dallas educator (and Blanton's friend) Lela Lee Williams became TSTA's leader. From 1944 to 1977, the presidency alternated between males and females, a reform long advocated by Blanton and other women members.[52]

Blanton's term in 1917 solidified the reputation she had gained through her textbooks and her Denton activities. Her work as TSTA president put her in contact with other well-known teachers and allowed her to form firsthand opinions of individuals she would encounter again when she sought the office of state superintendent in 1918, such as incumbent state superintendent and future adversary W. F. Doughty, who served on the association's Committee on Education Progress Within the State while Blanton was president. Blanton learned much about politics and education as the leader of TSTA, and clearly some of the opinions she espoused in future years about a "dominant ring" of male teachers, who opposed progressive changes in education, had their origins in her 1917 experiences. Blanton's activism for women in TSTA continued after her presidency ended, as she maintained her fight for a larger role for women and for rank-and-file teachers. Later, as state superintendent, she once had a public disagreement with publisher H. T. Musselman in his *Texas School Journal* over her advocacy of her friend Williams for the TSTA presidency. These experiences, especially the ones that occurred while she served as TSTA president, matured and seasoned her, prompting Blanton to write to Anna Pennybacker that 1917 had been the most trying year of her life.[53]

Blanton's relationship with Pennybacker formed another noteworthy element of her time as TSTA president. Pennybacker was a prominent Texas woman and very much the type of person whose competence, confidence, and prestige Blanton admired. Pennybacker's affiliation with educational issues in Texas included the publication, with her husband, of the first textbook on Texas history in 1888; fourteen years of teaching experience; and a position on the Executive Board of the Conference for Education in Texas.[54]

This group, which existed from 1907 to 1912, was the leading organization in Texas in the early twentieth century to advocate Progressive school reform. Similar to—but not officially part of—a larger movement of the same nature, which was then taking place throughout the South, the conference consisted of prominent educators working for such issues as rural school improvements, more adequate local school taxes, and a compulsory attendance law. Blanton, a member of the conference and "heartily in sympathy" with its purposes, no doubt admired Pennybacker for her leadership role in the group.[55]

Because of Pennybacker's presidencies of both the Texas Federation of Women's Clubs and the national General Federation of Women's Clubs, she was also well known to Texas women, such as Blanton, who were active in club work. Blanton and Pennybacker had begun corresponding with one another as early as 1915, discussing a possible visit to North Texas by Pennybacker, and when Pennybacker did visit Denton, she stayed with Blanton and the other women boarders in her home. By 1917, their letters had become frequent, covering issues of mutual interest, including suffrage, the political battle between Gov. James E. Ferguson and the University of Texas, and Blanton's new role in the TSTA. Although Pennybacker was only nine years her senior, Blanton held her in high esteem and regarded her as a mentor. After Ferguson's ouster from office, Blanton had hoped the new governor, William P. Hobby, would change the requirement that university regents had to be qualified voters and would appoint Pennybacker to that board. When Blanton organized her 1917 TSTA program, she selected Pennybacker as a featured speaker along with other nationally prominent women; Pennybacker also assisted Blanton in securing the appearance of Governor Hobby on the program.[56]

In 1918, Blanton and Pennybacker continued to discuss suffrage strategies, but Blanton also wrote Pennybacker increasingly about her own professional situation. Blanton's relationship with North Texas President Bruce had become uneasy as Blanton had heightened her outspoken advocacy of the suffrage campaign in Texas and her opposition to former governor Ferguson, political issues on which Bruce believed teachers should not publicly take stands. Blanton wanted to leave North Texas but hated to break up her home and leave her close companions in Denton. Although she received other job offers, Blanton became interested in a position in Denton's other school, the College of Industrial Arts (CIA), which would allow her to keep her home as well as provide an agreeable teaching position. Enlisting the help of Pennybacker, Blanton launched a behind-the-scenes campaign to make CIA president F. M. Bralley aware of her interest in the school and of her personal and professional qualifications. Her letters to Pennybacker during this time reveal Blanton's willingness to use the rivalries between the two male Denton college presidents to her own advantage. They also reveal her confidence in herself as a southern woman educator. "I think Mr. Bralley makes a mistake in filling up his school with so many Northern women," she wrote to Pennybacker on April 3, 1918, adding that these women lacked an interest in the school equal to that possessed by those who took pride in Texas and southern traditions.[57] This commitment to protect her state and region from outside influences, while at the same time working to improve its educational facilities, was consistent with the goals of Progressives throughout the South. And, like many Progressive women in the region, Blanton pursued these goals while maintaining the image of a proper southern female.[58] "Though a strong and most intelligent advocate of women and their rights, she belongs to that class peculiarly fitting to the South called ladies," the editors of the University of Texas alumni magazine, *The Alcalde,* wrote of Blanton in 1918.[59]

By the end of April, Blanton was convinced that Bralley was not sufficiently interested in hiring her, and, rather than risk humiliation, she turned her focus elsewhere. Considering political races for state superintendent and Congress, Blanton continued to confide in Pennybacker and seek her advice in long and detailed letters.[60] In the midst of an almost daily exchange of letters in May, 1918, Blanton acknowledged her debt to Pennybacker, noting that "I fear that you are finding it rather strenuous to be adviser to a person like me, who comes to you in all of her perplexities."[61]

Blanton's frequent correspondence with Pennybacker continued throughout her 1918 state superintendent campaign, despite the fact that many suffrage leaders, including Minnie Fisher Cunningham, resented Pennybacker's initial slow support of woman suffrage. After her election, Blanton provided details of her opponents' tactics to Pennybacker and also sought her advice on the many new decisions she faced. "I feel that the confidence and affection between us is such that neither need fear any misunderstanding by the other," she wrote to Pennybacker in August.[62] In the fall of 1918, when Blanton resigned from North Texas and moved to Austin to prepare to take office, she established residence with Emma Mitchell in Pennybacker's Whitis

Avenue home in Austin, while Pennybacker was involved with Chautauqua work in New York. The two women exchanged regular correspondence on both household and political matters. This housing arrangement ended in September, 1919, but Blanton and Pennybacker continued to write to each other throughout the 1920s and into the 1930s, although the regularity and intimacy declined as Blanton established herself as state superintendent and then, later, left the political arena.[63] Their relationship, however, had been critical for Blanton as she thought through her educational and political goals in 1918, and it had been no mere coincidence that she had turned to a prominent, successful, progressive, and yet in many ways traditional woman for such assistance. Moving from the teaching profession to statewide political office, Blanton benefited from Pennybacker's political experience and knowledge as well as her influence. Their relationship remained rather formal—in their letters they never used first names—but it was one based on trust, admiration, and shared beliefs, and there is a relaxed, comfortable tone in Blanton's letters to Pennybacker that is absent from her correspondence with male advisers and colleagues. As much as anyone, Pennybacker contributed as an adviser and mentor to Blanton's women-centered world at that important time of her life.[64]

Pennybacker exerted an especially profound influence on her because their relationship blossomed at a time of substantial change for Blanton, whose last few years in Denton had brought much professional success. Established and respected at North Texas, for both her teaching and publications, she broadened her reputation through her effective TSTA presidency. Her election as one of the vice-presidents of the National Education Association in 1917—the first of three terms she would serve in that position—coincided with her TSTA work and kept her name before prominent educational groups.[65]

Blanton had also witnessed her institution change in those years. By 1918, North Texas had matured from its early days as a teacher training school and had become an institution that offered the equivalent of a junior college education. It was Texas' premier normal school, and it was in the process of having its curriculum accredited at the full college level. An enrollment of more than one thousand students, a faculty of almost sixty, and expansions of buildings and library holdings demonstrated the school's growth.[66] The development of North Texas and Blanton's own professional growth were related; her work as a teacher, author, and educational leader brought recognition to the school, but simultaneously the growing college provided Blanton a respected base from which to work and view firsthand the needs, problems, and successes of education. Blanton often had professional disagreements with the school's president, Dr. Bruce, but his long tenure at North Texas, from 1906 to 1923, lent a stability and constancy to the school that benefited its students and faculty.[67]

Blanton's years in Denton had given her confidence, an opportunity to develop and articulate her ideas, and an extended period of time for personal and professional enjoyment. Those years were busy—extremely so by most anyone else's standards—but a relaxed spirit existed in Denton for Blanton that she had not experienced previously. With lessened family responsibilities, her salary allowed her to live comfortably, travel, attend graduate school in the summers, and build her own home. She immensely enjoyed sharing this home with close friends and taking part in Denton's intellectual and civic activities while happily pursuing her career. Yet, by 1918 Blanton's commitment to improve opportunities for both public schools and professional women made the suffrage issue and the fear of former governor Ferguson's return to office events of utmost concern. She believed that, in the meantime, she had reached an impasse with Dr. Bruce concerning her contribution to such causes. With her vision of social reform now clear, she began to consider other opportunities, and by mid-September of that year she had resigned from North Texas and moved to Austin to embark on a new venture.[68]

At this point, education and politics merged for Blanton in a way unique to both the state and its new women voters, providing her with both a broader audience and yet another challenging role as a woman from a traditional profession who sought progressive reform at an elite level previously dominated by males. In her newfound role in politics, as well as later in both her professional work at the University of Texas and her organizational efforts to found a society for women teachers, Blanton's experiences in Denton guided her. The teaching and leadership roles she had developed there were of paramount importance to her future, which also benefited from the maturation and articulation of her political concerns, specifically her desire to achieve more equalized professional opportunities for women teachers. Leaving Denton, the forty-eight-year-old Blanton took with her a unique perspective both as an educator and as a woman who enjoyed and found inspiration in competent, professional women similar to herself. Her ability to use that perspective, without alienating large elements of Texas' male leadership in educational and political arenas, formed a major aspect of her 1918 campaign and her subsequent four-year tenure as state superintendent of public instruction.

Politics and Education

1 9 1 8 - 2 2

It was not a casual choice that led the Denton instructor to attend the Texas Equal Suffrage Association's state convention in Austin in May, 1918. A strong supporter of the organization, Blanton eagerly wanted to stay informed of the unfolding political situation regarding woman suffrage and the effort to keep former Governor Ferguson from succeeding in his bid to regain office in the summer Democratic primary. She also had personal reasons for attending the meeting. Although not at all sure that she was ready to run for political office, Blanton was well aware of the interest others had in her as a candidate for state superintendent of public instruction, the top administrator of Texas public schools. Whatever her final decision regarding the race, she knew that the TESA meeting would be an excellent place to assess just how serious the interest in her was and how eager this important group might be to support her. Thus Blanton accepted the group's invitation to speak before them, and when she heard the members pass a unanimous resolution encouraging her to run for office, she had her answer.

On July 27, 1918, Texas voters, including white women exercising their recently attained right to vote in primaries, elected Annie Webb Blanton by an overwhelming margin as the Democratic candidate, and thus the ultimate victor, in the race for the office of state superintendent of public instruction.[1] As the first woman in Texas elected to statewide office, Blanton's campaign and election were closely tied to the suffrage movement in Texas, and benefited from both the newly enfranchised female voters and the ongoing fight for full suffrage.[2]

However, the election and subsequent tenure of Blanton as the state's top education official cannot be reduced simply to suffrage politics. As her experiences in Denton had demonstrated, Blanton had educational, political, and feminist ideals that went beyond women's attainment of voting rights. From 1918 through 1922, her personal and political agenda uniquely blended Texas Progressivism, reform feminism, and racial exclusivism, and her experiences chronicled both the opportunities and the limits of these elements.[3] By directly combining politics and education, Blanton sought to reduce the influence of politicians like James E. Ferguson and his friends in Texas schools, to capitalize on the potential of educated women in the electorate, and to make Texas morally conservative and socially progressive. She shared the southern Progressive ideal of pursuing redemptive forces in order to develop a better state, and she utilized, in particular, two important tenets of her region's white Progressivism to further her own goals: suffrage and a better school system. In her pursuits, Blanton pushed the line of gender discrimination back a considerable distance, but she did not obliterate it. She made noticeable improvements to Texas schools; yet problems remained. She helped create more female professional leadership opportunities; yet these efforts were always aimed at a very specific, and not particularly large, group of women. Indeed, all of Blanton's reform efforts were characterized by the racially exclusionary attitudes prevalent in her time; Blanton's work in politics, education, and women's emancipation never intended to reach beyond a white constituency.[4]

Blanton's election in July, 1918, followed a pivotal year of events in Texas politics. In September, 1917, the controversial Governor Ferguson had been forced to leave office after a lengthy fight with the University of Texas that had focused on Ferguson's mistrust of higher education officials there and their countercharges of his own financial improprieties and connections, during wartime, with the German-American alliance. When Ferguson vetoed the university's appropriations in June, 1917, he assured a showdown

Annie Webb Blanton in 1918, the year she ran for state superintendent of public instruction. (Photo courtesy Barker Texas History Center, University of Texas, Austin.)

with the state legislature. In September, the Senate, in session as a high court of impeachment, found Ferguson guilty on ten of twenty-one charges. Before the Senate could assess a penalty, however, Ferguson resigned on September 24, and Lt. Gov. William P. Hobby succeeded him.[5]

Despite his previous record against prohibition and his hardly strong stand on woman suffrage, Hobby's ascent to office represented victory for several Progressive elements in the state. Proponents of prohibition and woman suffrage saw in the new governor, if not clear strong support, at least an opportunity to pursue their causes with someone less outspoken on behalf of the opposition than Ferguson had been. Hobby's called session of the Thirty-fifth Legislature in February, 1918 — convened under some pressure from progressive Democrats — resulted in a statewide prohibition bill, special antiliquor and antiprostitution regulations for military zones, and passage of a primary suffrage law for women.[6]

Such Progressive issues joined Texas with other southern states seeking to improve the social order of their region while maintaining its basic cultural values. Suffrage, in particular, was proposed to bring deserving white women into the electorate and, thus, ensure white supremacy at the ballot box. The suffrage movement in the South (and in Texas), then, remained largely nonmilitant and worked within the confines of the racial orthodoxy of the time. Even with these contours, however, many males felt threatened by female voting rights and the idea of bringing women directly into the world of politics. Thus, the attainment of suffrage for women was not easy in any southern state, and Texas and Arkansas were the only southern states to succeed in offering women significant voting rights before passage of the Nineteenth Amendment to the U.S. Constitution in 1920.[7]

In Texas, the success of the primary suffrage bill in 1918 represented an important step, but not a final victory, for suffragists. From their earliest demands in 1868, this group's strength had been erratic and largely disorganized — until 1915, when the movement, known as the Texas Woman Suffrage Association, elected the effective and persuasive Minnie Fisher Cunningham as president. The next year the group changed its name to the Texas

Equal Suffrage Association (TESA), affiliated with the National American Woman Suffrage Association, and emphasized local grassroots support. After several failed legislative attempts to gain full voting rights, Texas suffragists in 1918 focused their efforts on primary suffrage, which would require only a simple legislative majority for passage and could serve as a starting point in attaining full suffrage. Since Texas was effectively a one-party state, primary voting rights would provide an important political entry point for women. Exercising hard work and persistence and benefiting from the absence of Ferguson from the governor's office, TESA succeeded in its bid.[8] The bill signed by Governor Hobby on March 26, 1918, gave white Texas women the right to vote in all primary elections and nominating conventions. It became effective June 26, leaving suffragists just seventeen days to register before the deadline for the July 27 primary (the act had exempted women from paying the required advanced poll tax); in those seventeen days, 386,000 Texas women registered to vote. Black women, however, were no part of this arrangement. Local party executives administered primaries and often barred blacks from participating. The suffragists were certainly unwilling to challenge the prevailing notion against black suffrage or take the political risk of encouraging black women to register to vote. Although some black women did register, it appears that none voted. Further, the primary suffrage bill required that each woman fill out her voter registration form in her own hand—a literacy test of sorts designed especially to keep illiterate black and Hispanic women from voting. They were presumed, as uneducated women, to be potential Ferguson supporters.[9]

With Ferguson's decision to enter the Democratic primary and run against Hobby for governor in the summer of 1918, as well as the desire of Texas Progressives to see prohibition and full suffrage enacted nationwide, the primary vote on July 27 was pivotal. In the governor's race, the newly enfranchised women, along with male prohibitionists, aligned with Hobby against the irrepressible Ferguson, whom they saw as the "implacable foe of woman suffrage and of every great moral issue for which women stood."[10] Races for other statewide offices exhibited similar themes.

Soon after Hobby had signed the primary suffrage law, Blanton, contemplating a change of employment anyway, was encouraged by friends, the Texas Congress of Mothers, and suffrage leader Cunningham to enter the political arena by running for state superintendent. By this time, Blanton's experiences as a public school teacher, college professor, author, and former state teachers' association president had made her known as one of Texas' more prominent educators.[11] She also was attuned to the political situation in Texas and was personally interested in it. Hobby was a great hero to her because he had saved the University of Texas from Ferguson's ongoing interference.[12] Ferguson was no friend of Progressive reformers in Texas, and Blanton sympathized with those who opposed his antisuffrage and antiprohibition efforts, resented his connections to the powerful brewery industry, and feared his appeals to poorer, less educated, rural Texans. Yet her opposition to the former governor and his populist brand of politics also focused on his interference with her alma mater and his association with numerous male secondary school administrators, as well as her fear that Ferguson would continue to garner support from people who either did not know any better or who had selfish motives. "He has a wonderful power over a certain class of people, and they are so numerous," she wrote Cunningham on May 10, 1918. And to Anna Pennybacker she noted that Ferguson was "lining up the vicious, the ignorant, the prejudiced to his support" and was campaigning specifically against educated people.[13]

Ferguson's attitude regarding the University of Texas was distinct from his concern for public schools. Upon becoming governor in January, 1915, he had successfully pursued his goal to improve public schools, particularly rural facilities. Numerous educational reforms had been passed by the legislature because of the joint efforts by Ferguson and then–state superintendent W. F. Doughty. These results were not surprising to most public educators; early in 1915, the *Texas School Journal* editorialized about the "great service for the cause of education" expected from the new governor and Superintendent Doughty. Despite Ferguson's decent public school reform record, Blanton nevertheless considered his interference at the university too serious to overlook and believed it indicated a potential for political disruption in educational matters whenever he held office. Her opposition to Ferguson was reinforced by her suspicions of his desire to keep Texas schools under the control of a few powerful males. Therefore, even though Blanton favored Ferguson's general educational reforms, his approach to a few specific educational issues incurred her opposition and allowed her to join willingly with those Progressives who fought Ferguson's antisuffrage and antiprohibition stances.[14]

Blanton formed her views on Ferguson during her time as president of the state teachers' association and articulated them—albeit somewhat obliquely—throughout 1917 and 1918. She argued that Ferguson and certain school administrators clearly were operating together to keep the Texas school system under their control, although her attacks on this group were vague and without specific evidence. When she decided to run for office, she explained that she was doing so in order to allow Texas to have a state superintendent who was not sympathetic to Ferguson and who would remove schools from the mire of politics, but again she did not elaborate. She accused Doughty of being close to Ferguson and of building up a strong political machine, but she specified no other names or activities related to this group.[15] She had decided to campaign largely because of her desire to rid Texas of "Fergusonism," and during the race Blanton complained, again without elaboration, that Ferguson and his men were trying to defeat her brother in his congressional race as a means to hurt her.[16] A few months before taking office, she again made reference to the Ferguson machine, this time in a letter to Pennybacker: "There is a regular 'line-up' against me of certain school men who are determined now to try to take away from the State Department [of Education] the powers they have been trying to give it in the past."[17]

Blanton certainly had no reason to believe that Ferguson, Doughty, or many other male school leaders shared her desire to improve the status of women teachers and to increase a sense of democracy in the teaching profession, themes she publicly had articulated as president of the state teachers' association. However, it is difficult to ascertain whether her accusations rested on actual efforts that these men had made to hurt her or more on her perceptions of their intentions.

While in Denton, Blanton endorsed the efforts of the Texas Equal Suffrage Association because she believed woman suffrage would allow for the development of better-educated voters and would thus keep out of office men such as Ferguson. "You and I are one in purpose," she wrote to TESA president Minnie Fisher Cunningham in August, 1917.[18] That purpose was to attain suffrage as a means ultimately to benefit society. In the American woman suffrage movement after 1900, this argument that extended voting rights would result in an improved society took precedence over claims of the injustice of disenfranchisement.[19] While she did want to end unfairness and inequalities, Blanton often chose, as an advocate of woman suffrage, to emphasize the usefulness of women's votes in improving the current state of government. She believed woman suffrage could enhance patriotism, education, and leadership—all elements essential to improve society— if only women would use their voting rights wisely.[20] Soon after Texas women had achieved primary suffrage, she noted to Cunningham that woman suffrage was now "on trial" and that its justification would come only with women's correct voting. She was concerned that women could be captivated by the wrong influences. "Indifferent, unthinking women won't vote right. I fear the Ferguson influence," Blanton wrote to Cunningham in the spring of 1918.[21] In her attempts to educate new voters, Blanton addressed women in Denton, explaining how to understand election issues and how to mark a ballot.[22] Once in office, she campaigned for adoption of the state amendments for prohibition and full suffrage, and against the influences she considered negative, noting to Pennybacker: "The campaigns are going well. I have spoken for both over the state, so know the general sentiment. But, of course, there is doubt. The alien, the pro-German, the anti will vote against us."[23] Like many other Progressives in Texas, the South, and throughout the United States, Blanton believed that the quality of voters—who, in her mind, would be educated, native, white, middle- and upper-class citizens of both sexes—remained more important than simply having a numerous electorate.[24]

Behind Blanton's desire for women to demonstrate their capabilities as voters lay a feminist ideology with similar tenets. Blanton's general interest in equality for women derived from her family background and personal experiences, which influenced and reinforced her recognition of women's abilities. Basic to her convictions was the desire to bring women into positions of leadership so they could improve the society in which they lived, not revolutionize it. When she became involved in the movement to gain voting rights for women in Texas, she found her closest allies in Pennybacker and Cunningham, middle-class, moderate voices in the state's suffrage organization.[25]

As a professional educator she knew that the lowest salaries for teachers routinely went to women. She had often encountered opposition as TSTA president simply because she was female. She was aware of the limits traditionally encountered by women who wished to advance from the classroom to administrative positions. Such discriminations, based on gender rather than ability, offended Blanton, and she sought to end them.[26] Not long after her election as state superintendent, Blanton alluded to these problems to a group of teachers: "Most women who have had to face the world alone have found themselves up against a solid wall of sex prejudice. There are some of us who have climbed that wall, and we are stretching out our hands to those who are still struggling after us; and we shall never be satisfied until it is beaten down forever."[27]

As a southern Progressive, however, Blanton set significant limitations on this feminist call. Her approach, in fact elitist and discriminating, required women to prove their competence, before they could enjoy the same opportunities as men. In a clear sense, equality was for Blanton an earned privilege rather than an inherent right.

Blanton, then, saw the need to improve opportunities for women within a narrow context. Because she maintained this specific focus, Blanton avoided many of the difficult problems commonly associated with uniting different types of women into a broad, common movement for equality. Furthermore, throughout her life she found little relevance in the contemporary debates concerning feminism, such as whether it was still necessary or whether it offered only a socially dangerous obliteration of sexual differences. Blanton's feminism arose from more practical concerns; it was narrowly defined but deeply believed, simple in concept but enduringly held, and its origins were intensely personal. She considered herself a committed professional who had proven her abilities as an educator to be equal or even superior to those of her male colleagues. She believed she should therefore have access to every opportunity provided male educators. Blanton's womanhood meant many things to her, but never inferiority. Building upon observations of her own situation, Blanton applied the same litmus test to other white women: if they had proven themselves, they deserved equality, which she was determined to help them achieve. Recognizing and rewarding female competence, Blanton thought, would ultimately bring about the end of unfair situations as well as the riddance of undeserving males, such as Ferguson and his associates, all of which would result in an improved society. [28]

Blanton's personal and political means to pursue her feminist perspectives lay in education—both as a profession and a practice. As her 1916 teachers' association speech demonstrated, she understood the importance of substantive equality rather than mere token elections or achievements. She also took advantage of the changes in the South early in this century, which, along with the suffrage movement, provided women increased choices in nondomestic endeavors. As women's clubs and other self-improvement organizations began to flourish, the idea that women could contribute to society—by using their intellectual capacities and moving beyond the literal bounds of domesticity—was gradually reaching social acceptance in the South, and Blanton was one of many southern women to avail herself of this social transformation. By cooperating with the suffragists, while directing most of her efforts into her activities as a professional educator, Blanton created her own distinctive brand of feminism and spent the remainder of her life extending its potential to those of her choosing. [29]

Ironically, her faculty position at North Texas became an obstacle to her political and educational activism in 1917 and 1918, when President Bruce stipulated that no representative of North

Texas could participate in any political movements, including woman suffrage. Bruce's motivations for his decision remain unclear, but he may have been following the lead of other university presidents, such as James Taylor at Vassar, who believed that female educators' participation in the suffrage fight on campus would be inconsistent with the exemplary role models they were supposed to provide. Whatever the causes for Bruce's decision, Blanton struggled with it. The link between improving opportunities for women teachers and gaining voting rights for women was obvious to her. She wanted to work for suffrage because she was eager for good women voters to be able to broaden their contribution to society and, in particular, to better the Texas school system. She also believed woman suffrage was morally correct and would help ensure Ferguson's defeat, which in turn would afford greater democracy within the teaching profession.[30]

Initially she attempted to conduct her suffrage work in ways she thought would be acceptable. She sent letters to the Texas congressional delegation in Washington, but not to the state legislators, who had a more direct hand in administering North Texas. She also routinely told Cunningham that her suffrage work had to remain limited: she could neither organize a suffrage society at North Texas nor become an officer in any such society, unless she chose to resign from her teaching position. However, for a woman who rarely spent time doubting the correctness of her convictions, this arrangement, imposed by a male superior, was difficult and uncomfortable.[31] By March, 1918, the month the primary suffrage law was signed, Blanton had become exasperated. She wrote to Cunningham, "I am not going to sit back any longer with a matter like this at stake. I don't believe anyone has a right to hamper me in such a matter, and, if I lose my position thereby—so be it—I can get another."[32] The next month Blanton wrote to Pennybacker, "I've made up my mind that Dr. Bruce has no right to keep me from working for good government in Texas, so I am losing no chance of lining up the women, wherever I speak, for Hobby." She also told Pennybacker that she was considering several teaching offers from other schools, but that regardless of her decision, she would leave North Texas because "things will never be pleasant for me again here."[33]

Blanton acknowledged to Pennybacker early in April that suffragists and the Mother's Congress had urged her to enter the race for state superintendent. Although she admitted that she aspired to be superintendent someday, she was not certain that women should run for office until they had proven their ability to vote wisely. Blanton's correspondence for the next two months shows her cautiously considering her next move. She wrote about her consideration of seeking a position at the College of Industrial Arts, so that she could keep the home she had built in Denton. She said that she did not consider herself financially set to undertake a statewide race. She also worried that her obvious pro-university stance might bring out strong Ferguson supporters to vote against her. She feared the physical and emotional rigors of the contest, as well as what opponents might make of her lack of degrees beyond the Bachelor's level. On the other hand, she considered the encouragement she had received in Denton to run for U.S. Congress, where she would be able to advocate educational efforts in a larger arena and to work for such measures as the establishment of the Bureau of Education as a cabinet-level agency.[34] The uncertain and often contradictory nature of her correspondence at this time shows both her eagerness to delve into politics and her fear of what such an undertaking might require. Blanton did not doubt that she could contribute to the advancement of her causes, but she was unsure of what was the best way to proceed. She wrote to Cunningham on May 10, "If I succeeded, I might help the woman's cause, because I have studied public questions all my life. But I honestly think that, if I fail, as is probable, my failure would injure the woman's cause in Texas."[35]

Meanwhile Cunningham had issued an invitation for Blanton to speak at the TESA state convention in Austin in May of 1918. The invitation indicated the organization's intention to draft Blanton for office, regardless of her own doubts. "Drafting" Blanton was an astute move for the suffragists and reflected their desire both to contribute to and benefit from the various political concerns facing voters in 1918. Cunningham had promised to mobilize women for Hobby in return for the primary suffrage bill, and getting Blanton on the ballot seemed a tangible way to help do that.[36]

Complex political maneuverings contributed to the suffragists' support of Blanton, but their decision to make her their candidate was logical. She was professionally qualified to be state superintendent and had already determined to leave North Texas. In addition, having a woman on the primary ballot seemed a plausible way to inspire newly enfranchised Texas women to vote — mainly to help Hobby win and thus to keep Ferguson out of office. Blanton's opposition to Ferguson, even if ideologically based as much on educational issues as on suffrage, aligned her politically with TESA. Since Blanton was already well known among teachers, supporters hoped that she could appeal to this element of educated women who also would then vote for Hobby. She also had revealed to the suffragists that she even had the ability to reach, through a secret organization, a large group of influential women teachers. And her brother's already demonstrated commitment to work for national suffrage and prohibition in the U.S. Congress must have been at least an indirect consideration in Blanton's selection. Election of a woman to statewide office clearly would help the suffragists maintain a visible campaign for full suffrage. Yet, by championing a woman to head Texas schools, they exhibited political caution by claiming an area that was already largely a female domain. Rather than seek to place a woman in office in a field traditionally associated only with men, they aimed instead to extend female influence by placing a woman at the head of a profession in which she already had a foothold. As one member of the Austin Equal Suffrage Association later said, "It is especially fitting that the first elective office held by a woman should be an educational one, since women are, after all, the chief educators of our youth." This strategy had already been successful in several western states, including Colorado and Washington, where women had been elected to the office of state superintendent.[37]

On May 13, 1918, TESA unanimously adopted a resolution urging Blanton to run for state superintendent. Citing women's ongoing interest in education, a predominant majority of females in the teaching profession, and Blanton's splendid qualifications, the resolution specified that a committee call on Blanton and ask that she enter the race. Present at the meeting, Blanton seized the drama of the moment and affirmed that, despite whatever doubts she might have had earlier, she could not decline TESA's call to patriotic duty for Texas. On June 1, with the primary less than two months away, she filed for office.[38]

Blanton campaigned as a traditional southern Democrat. As she put it: "I am a Democrat, first, because in my opinion, this party has always stood, more than any other, for the rights of the great masses of the people of America. Second, I am a Democrat because I am a believer in the principle of taxation for necessary revenue only. Third, I suppose the fact that I am a loyal Southerner and still cherish the best ideals of the Old South has had some influence in making me a Democrat."[39] Her form of southern Progressivism encompassed the elements that historian Dewey Grantham has defined as a reconciliation of tradition and progress, propelled by activism. It derived from a strong sense of democracy, patriotism, public service, feminism, and education, all of which helped create a belief that government could be improved. Blanton combined politics and education in order to work for what she believed would be a cleaner, more stable government. In this government certain "influences" perceived to be detrimental were minimized: blacks, the liquor interests, German Americans, and other non-native groups. Nonetheless this government needed to broaden its allowance for women's participation — at least to a select group of women. With the "wrong" influences out and the "right" white women in, Blanton believed the state's heritage of democracy would remain intact. Her role as a professional educator provided her the avenue to pursue these goals and the forum to articulate them.[40]

The campaign for state superintendent unfolding that summer featured most of the then-predominant Progressive issues in Texas: woman suffrage, prohibition, anti-Fergusonism, and education. The suffrage association, guided primarily by Cunningham and Professor Alexander Caswell Ellis of the University of Texas, chose to focus exclusively on Blanton's opponent, incumbent superintendent W. F. Doughty. A Democrat from Falls County, Doughty had been appointed state superintendent in 1913 by Gov. O. B. Colquitt to fill an unexpired term and then had been elected in his own right in 1914 and 1916.[41] Until the suffragists' challenge, Doughty had aroused little opposition as superintendent and had successfully worked with the legislature for passage of several education bills. His cooperation with Governor Ferguson had resulted in numerous Progressive educational measures and, therefore, was not widely perceived as a negative factor. Moreover, as a University of Texas alumnus, he did not share Ferguson's reputation as hostile to that institution. When he announced his bid for reelection in December, 1917, the *Texas School Journal* proclaimed that he should be returned to office without opposition because "the record of Doughty's work is unassailable."[42]

Ellis and Cunningham disagreed. Relying on public records from a 1915 Sulphur Springs court case that the State of Texas had brought against seven Texas brewery companies, Ellis and Cunningham built their own case to suggest that Doughty himself was connected to the liquor trusts. They focused on two brief, 1914 letters from Otto Wahrmund, president of the San Antonio Brewing Association and a member of the state legislature. One letter to liquor dealer J. J. Elliott of Thorndale included a reference to Doughty as "o.k. and our friend." The other, to Doughty himself, expressed admiration for the superintendent.[43] The suffrage association considered the implications certain: despite Doughty's professed endorsement of statewide prohibition, he appeared to be a friend of the brewers—meaning he probably took their money and thus protected their interests. Aside from his having misrepresented his views, which the suffragists deeply resented, Doughty's relationship with brewers in the state tainted him in the women's eyes by connecting him to three of the greatest evils known to the suffragists: Germany (through Wahrmund), both the wartime enemy and a country with direct ties to the brewing industry; alcohol; and Jim Ferguson, one of the state's best-known antiprohibitionists and a friend of the brewers. As Cunningham wrote to a rather bewildered Doughty, who believed that the suffragists should support him because of his educational record and not disrupt the progress being made, "We felt it inconceivable that the women of Texas should help elect to that position, with their first ballot, a man who subordinated the interests of the educational system of the state to the Brewers Association."[44]

By focusing on Doughty's apparent liquor connection, Cunningham and Ellis set a tone for the campaign that sometimes obscured Blanton's role in the race. It is possible that TESA leaders had had the court records before they approached Blanton to run, and thus had determined to defeat Doughty before deciding who was the most appropriate candidate to support in his stead. After Blanton was in the race, Cunningham hinted that it was paramount to remove Doughty from the office that set the "standards of ideals to be taught the youth of the land."[45] Caswell Ellis was more direct, writing to Cunningham that the "fact that Miss Blanton is very competent is actually a mere incident" and was not itself the reason for removing Doughty from office.[46] For Cunningham and Ellis, the key objectives in the race were garnering support for Hobby and, at the same time, removing Doughty from office, which would then directly decrease the influence of Ferguson and antiprohibition forces in the state. Cunningham and Ellis naturally sought a successor to Doughty who would be sympathetic to their cause and would appeal to the new women voters, but they knew that, in order to defeat the incumbent, they could not rely upon a campaign that focused exclusively on the issues of education, woman suffrage, and competence.

Ellis, who contributed his political and educational experience to Blanton's campaign, sincerely advocated woman suffrage and ardently opposed Jim Ferguson. In July, 1917, Ellis had been dismissed from his position in the University of Texas' school of education by the board of regents at Ferguson's behest on account of Ellis's work in extension (or continuing) education, which the governor considered inappropriate. Reinstated three months later by new Governor Hobby, Ellis, like many University of Texas supporters, had no difficulty opposing Ferguson or anyone possibly connected to him.[47]

In Blanton's campaign, he played a critical role in the development of strategy and the management of campaign finances. He supervised the writing and distribution of campaign literature and served as an unofficial liaison between the Blanton and Hobby campaigns.[48] When campaign finances became tight, he sent his wife and Austin suffragist Jane McCallum to visit pioneer Texas suffragist and San Antonio philanthropist Eleanor Brackenridge for "a thousand or two." A week later, Cunningham forwarded Brackenridge's one thousand dollars to Blanton for use in the campaign.[49] Ellis also admonished Blanton to toughen her efforts and repeatedly reminded Cunningham to keep the focus on Doughty and the brewers. When he thought that Blanton's efforts lacked the directness needed for a race of that nature, he reminded Cunningham that he had "advised Miss Blanton not to run unless she was willing to sail in with gloves off."[50] Two weeks before the primary, Ellis reemphasized to Cunningham the need for Blanton to avoid issues people were not familiar with: "Not one person in ten cares whether Doughty stuck to his University or not. Practically nobody but 'us women' cared whether he employed all men or not. And lots of men are very anxious not to start the idea that the state superintendent must always be a woman. . . . In my opinion we have just one thing to do, that is to prove Doughty unfit. To do this only one thing is needed, that is to show that he is untruthful and is cheek-by-jowl with Jim Ferguson and the German-American brewers. . . . Get one idea in their heads and harp on it."[51]

Ellis's advice and influence kept the campaign focused, and Cunningham willingly followed his suggestions. Blanton generally accepted this strategy, but she also maintained her own agenda throughout the race. She kept her headquarters in Denton, where she had strong local support and could be independent from Cunningham in Houston and Ellis in Austin. By visiting five to seven towns a week, she spoke to a much broader audience and campaigned in a much more open manner than Ellis preferred, and she refused to be merely an ornament in the race. When Dallas suffragists cut short her address so that a male judge could speak, she fired off a letter to Cunningham, indignantly noting that she "had not expected them to sacrifice me to any man."[52] She also campaigned against a third candidate in the race, Brandon Trussell of Wise County. When Trussell labelled Blanton "a tool of others," she angrily responded with a summary of her record of independence as a teacher and as president of the state teachers' association. She also complained of Trussell's accusation that Blanton's boss, Dr. Bruce, had brought her into the race simply to be a spoiler, to ensure Doughty's victory over Trussell. Although Blanton and Bruce had differences of opinions on various issues and even though he did not support her candidacy, Bruce denied Trussell's charge, which clearly appears to have been a desperate and failed attempt by Trussell to improve his own election chances.[53]

Rather than directly challenge the advice of Cunningham and Ellis, Blanton built on it, maintaining her own priorities in the race in the process. In her campaign speeches and advertisements, she first noted that she had earned the right to run for the office, explaining that she was a capable candidate and that women already had proven their abilities in this office in other states. She then argued that woman suffrage benefited everyone because it helped offset the loss of male voters, a result of the war, by enfranchising an equally loyal patriotic group. Next, in attacking Doughty, she claimed that he had neglected democracy during his tenure by failing to appoint women to key positions, then focused on his connection with the brewers. Her speeches always included a statement about her strong desire to break up what she perceived as a male-dominated teachers' machine in Texas, and she usually mentioned a desire to remove politics from education and to return the focus to improving the welfare of schools. Other regular features of her campaign speeches included tributes to Hobby and criticism of Ferguson, whom she accused of running for governor illegally and being unfit for office. Blanton's willingness to fight hard in the race was balanced by campaign literature that promoted her "sympathetic understanding of the teacher's viewpoint" and her attributes as a "womanly woman."[54] Altogether, her speeches reflected her feminist persuasions: the importance of women's professional competence, the political and social dangers of incompetent men, and a comfortable acknowledgment of her own womanhood.

Doughty's late, ineffective strategies and countercharges inadvertently aided Blanton and her advisors. The suffragists' aggressive attack and Blanton's strong candidacy created a shock from which the incumbent never recovered. His refusal to announce his choice for governor because he wanted to be able to work with the winner caused him first to appear to favor Ferguson, then to look like an opportunist when he announced for Hobby after it became clear that Hobby would win. Doughty suggested that, since Blanton had written textbooks and thus could not serve on the State Text Book Board, she was also ineligible to be state superintendent, an argument that was legally incorrect. He maintained that his correspondence with Otto Wahrmund had been the simple result of a form letter sent to all Texas legislators and indicated no personal connections to the brewing industry. Blanton pointed out that for a statewide prohibitionist to be labeled "o.k." by a known "wet" implied something amiss, and then, further leveling an even more personal attack that undoubtedly appealed to many patriotic Texans during wartime, she noted that she herself had no "hyphenated" (meaning German-American) connections. A desperate Doughty tried other charges. He accused Blanton of opposing rural school aid, of being an atheist, of being immoral, and of hating men, but because these allegations implied notions about Blanton that not only had no basis in fact but which her life refuted, they had little impact.[55]

Doughty's best campaign tool was his record in office. Educational standards in Texas had improved during his tenure, and his leadership had proven instrumental in the passage of numerous important reform measures. He had also drafted a kindergarten bill for the Texas Federation of Women's Clubs, a group in which Blanton and other suffragists were active. However, such successes were not enough to enable him to cast off the liquor albatross that suffragists had hung around his neck in 1918. At the height of the war, the suffrage association made a successful appeal for the patriotic, prohibitionist, anti-Ferguson female vote. Blanton's tireless campaigning and personal commitment to win —she had invested in the race her own savings of fifty-five hundred dollars—and the suffrage association's persistent attack on Doughty ensured victory.[56] A TESA brochure for Blanton asked, "Shall the Fathers and Mothers of Texas or the Brewers and German-American Alliance O.K. Our State Superintendent of

Public Instruction?"[57] On July 27, 1918, Texas voters favored, not surprisingly, the fathers and mothers. Blanton easily won her race. More than six hundred thousand Texans cast their votes, and Blanton received nearly seventy thousand votes more than Doughty and Trussell combined. She joined Hobby, who defeated Ferguson, and other successful suffrage-backed candidates to provide the newly enfranchised women voters a sense of success, since victory in the July Democratic primary assured, in practice, election in November, even without the aid of women voters. Clearly, it was significant that a woman had been elected so soon after women had attained primary suffrage. Blanton's success demonstrated the suffrage movement's persistence, ability to learn from previous failures, and increasing political savvy. If, however, suffrage politics and Blanton won in 1918, victory came somewhat at the cost of a clearly articulated educational platform. During the campaign both Blanton and the TESA failed to address the crucial issues that the next state superintendent would face. With new educational laws in place, the challenge ahead would be the efficient, fair implementation of that legislation. Doughty realized that, but his slow response to campaign attacks, as well as the controversies that continued to swirl around him, disabled him.[58]

As Texas educator H. T. Musselman pointed out, on issues of a purely educational nature, Blanton and Doughty had few major differences, a fact that the suffrage association intentionally obscured in the course of the campaign. Musselman did not doubt Blanton's qualifications for office, but he thought that her appeal to the newly enfranchised women voters—summed up by an anonymous "clever" Texas woman who said, "This time we will vote en masse; next time we will think over the matter"— indicated that the support Blanton would have as state superintendent was based less on a mandate for a new direction in educational procedures than on her gender and her successful prohibition-backed campaign.[59] Ironically, the Progressive support that had helped to elect Blanton would also ensure that the educational efforts begun by Ferguson and Doughty would be continued. For not the first or last time in Texas political campaigns, attention to the personalities of the candidates and emotional calls for patriotism concealed a full discussion of the critical issues that would face the ultimate victor.

The ongoing educational reforms in Texas were central to these issues and part of a more comprehensive campaign in which Progressives in the southern United States had been engaged since the beginning of the century. The Conference for Education in the South sought solutions to such basic problems in the region as short school terms, low enrollment, limited funding, and low teacher salaries; universal education—meaning extension of educational reforms to blacks—was also important to the group, but with an emphasis on industrial education for blacks. Although Texas did not directly participate in the Conference or its Southern Education Board, it pursued a generally similar course of reform through the activities of various groups, including the Conference for Education in Texas, the Congress of Mothers, and the Texas State Teachers Association. Under Doughty's and Ferguson's direction in 1915, the state had legislated free textbooks, higher taxes for schools, compulsory attendance, and aid to rural schools. After 1915, Doughty worked to attain voter approval of the new laws and then to organize the necessary administrative structure for the implementation of each reform. This work had been his primary concern before the voters replaced him with Blanton.[60]

Despite the gains achieved in 1915, most educators in Texas, including both Doughty and Blanton, realized that what had been accomplished was long overdue and that much school reform work remained to be done. Thus, when Blanton assumed office, she not only inherited considerable administrative work that needed completion but also faced the challenge of establishing her own direction of reform while continuing the improvements to schools already begun. Her official duties, for which she received four thousand dollars a year, included administering school laws, supervising record-keeping and other work of subordinate school officials, approving state school finances, and staying informed of educational progress throughout the state.[61]

Cognizant of what had gone unsaid in the election race, Blanton was eager to establish her agenda once the campaign had ended. She first promised to work for equal opportunity and equal service for men and women teachers, to keep politics out of education, to harmonize educational forces, and to improve teacher salaries. Her negative references to the teachers' machine were common. "You know, the heads of most of the state schools don't love me, because I broke up their ring and because I am using my influence and office for better things for the teachers," she wrote Pennybacker soon after taking office.[62] Blanton argued that this ring threatened educational progress in Texas. She believed, based on her teachers' association presidency, that their interests lay in weakening the State Department of Education, hurting the University of Texas, turning textbook selections into a fraud, and blocking equal rights for women. Her convictions on this matter were clear, though again she offered no specific evidence to substantiate her claims. The claims probably resulted at least in part from Blanton's meeting resistance from common school districts that feared an overly powerful statewide educational administration. The "ring" may have referred to more than one group, although she consistently seemed to place Ferguson there. To Blanton, the goals of her opponents seemed more important than the reasons they opposed her.

Democracy and equality became her watchwords as state superintendent, and she was sincerely concerned with providing a sense of dignity to the classroom teacher, particularly the female teacher. Blanton told members of the state teachers' association in 1919 that the old-maid schoolteacher, who had influenced the American soldier during his most formative years, was just as responsible for helping to win the war as were parents or wives. To the National Education Association the same year, she stated that she found it hard to see any professional occupation as having more importance than the training of the children of America, but that she also thought the teaching profession needed to be more democratic.[63] As she put it, "The Creator did not make brains hereditary in the masculine line only. When we struggle to abolish sex distinctions in wage earning and in government, we are acting on the same principle which the world war was fought to maintain—that might and power do not constitute justice and right."[64] The democracy she referred to remained limited and was not meant to apply to black teachers—male or female. This prejudice was natural to her instincts and heritage, and there is no indication that she was troubled by racially limited democracy.[65]

Blanton referred often to opportunities for women and the development of strong women teachers. Having won the ballot had not guaranteed women equal opportunities in the professions; the teaching field remained riddled with discriminatory situations, including lower salaries for women and barriers to advancing to administrative positions. However, Blanton believed this could be changed if efforts were made gradually, tactfully, and persistently. While in office, she neglected no opportunities to advocate such changes and to encourage an esprit de corps for deserving women teachers. She admonished women deans to teach future female teachers that "no woman achieves man's respect who is a traitor to her own sex." Continuing to emphasize the theme of gender unity, she added, "One who labors with a wholly selfish motive is an ingrate to the pioneers of the past who paved the way for her own achievement, and . . . is a slacker in the battle for the progress of the future."[66]

Blanton appointed an equal number of men and women to head divisions in the State Department of Education, and she required state normal schools to do the same for their summer examiners. Blanton did not recognize normal schools that did not comply, so they could not hold their summer sessions. Because she encouraged women to seek leadership roles in the profession, and because she used her office to urge local districts to better utilize women teachers, the number of women who served on school boards and as school board officers and superintendents of county and independent school districts greatly increased while she was in office. Despite the potential controversy that such changes might have generated, no evidence of overt opposition to Blanton's efforts exists, possibly because women's role in school leadership had increased during the war, paving the way for more ready acceptance.[67] Equalizing salaries between males and females proved difficult, however, and Blanton was unable to attain passage of legislation that would provide sufficient penalty to discourage pay discrimination in public schools. This situation was frustrating for a professional and feminist such as Blanton. "While the differences in the salaries of men and women teachers is not, on the whole, commensurate with the difference in training, all women are, I think, willing to concede that no individual woman should demand pay equal to that of men teachers in similar positions, unless her scholastic training and experience are equal to theirs. It is the payment of better salaries to men of inferior qualifications that arouses dissatisfaction and resentment in the heart of the woman teacher," she wrote soon after leaving office.[68]

When Blanton entered office, the Russell Sage Foundation's ranking of Texas for education was thirty-ninth in the nation, largely because of low teacher salaries and low school attendance rates. Blanton's efforts resulted in raising Texas' rank to thirty-fourth in 1922, a feat which indicated that she had successfully kept alive the reform program in the state's schools, but had not made revolutionary changes.[69]

Neither the teachers' machine nor other political groups appear to have affected her efforts in any substantial way. The machine may have been less threatening than Blanton acknowledged, and others may have been indifferent, according to a 1918 editorial in the *Texas School Journal:* "The professional politicians care nothing about school offices. Say what you will, the fact is these offices are held in low esteem by the average politician. The rule is, therefore, that these politicians are perfectly willing for a woman to have the office of state superintendent so long as the women do not seek any other offices."[70]

Despite such perceptions of the office, Blanton approached her job in her usual diligent manner and left a substantial record of Progressive improvement in Texas education. Raising teacher salaries was an ongoing concern for her, and she helped bring about an average increase in annual salaries from $570 to $877 during her four years in office, an increase of 54 percent.[71] Blanton pressed for 100 percent increases because she feared the effects of having inferior teachers. "If the future of our state is to be worthy of its glorious past, we must vitalize our schools. Texas people must show themselves unwilling to accept for the school room the inferior and the untrained. Our children must be taught by the best," she said in 1920.[72]

She successfully worked to obtain an amendment to the free textbook law, which reorganized the distribution process, changed adoption procedures, and included a bond provision so that the average cost of books per child to school districts dropped from $3.47 in 1919 to $0.80 in 1922. In rural education, an area of special interest to the former Pine Springs teacher, she achieved an increased amount of special appropriations, a greater number of consolidated schools, a reduced number of one-teacher schools, and an increase in the number of homes provided to rural teachers by their schools.

Under Blanton's direction, the Department of Education increased its ranks from twenty-six to sixty employees, with two divisions added and staff increases in several existing ones. The revision of certification laws during her tenure allowed teachers to select a subject for examination for each grade of certification and to disallow any person from serving as a local school superintendent without a certificate. With her assistance, the state passed legislation that lengthened school terms from an average of 117.8 to 136.5 days per year. She enforced the 1915 compulsory attendance law, with the result that enrollment rose from 87.4 percent of children in the scholastic census of 1918–19 to 93.4 percent in 1921–22. Blanton implemented a plan to classify and to affiliate elementary schools so that standardization could be achieved in these schools in much the same way that accreditation aided high schools and colleges. In 1920, she served on an educational advisory committee appointed by Governor Hobby, which made recommendations that eventually led to a statewide survey of Texas schools in 1923 and 1924.[73]

Prior to her election, Blanton had advocated the election of county superintendents by county boards of education, rather than the general public, because she believed that this would reduce political involvement in educational matters and equalize the quality of superintendents between cities, where they were appointed, and counties. However, in her campaign of 1918, she approved maintaining the general election of the state superintendent because she believed the office's wide appointive powers and the need to keep individual terms shorter made election necessary and that programs should be subjected to regular public approval. Once in office, Blanton changed her opinion on this issue, arguing for the selection of the state superintendent by a state board of public school regents and a voluntary departure from office after four years. However, neither the county nor state superintendencies became appointive during her tenure.[74]

Blanton shared the prevalent attitude of her time that racially segregated schools were socially and educationally appropriate. Soon after leaving office, she wrote that schools for black children could never be as efficient as schools for whites, regardless of the effort made to improve them.[75] Nevertheless, during her tenure she did use funding from the General Education Board in New York to add to the rural education division of the Department of Education a supervisor and stenographer for black schools. Their work focused on finding funding sources for black schools and encouraging these institutions toward self-improvement. Blanton summarized her attitude toward black education in 1923, when she wrote of the supervisor for black schools: "Perhaps his most important work is to arouse the negroes to efforts towards self-help in the improvement of their own schools. To aid them to help themselves, and to arouse their pride in their own schools, is a more important service than that of assigning to them temporary donations."[76] Blanton's approach indicated her realization that education for black students needed attention but showed also how minimal was her involvement in this serious problem. As with the General Education Board funds, Blanton tended to permit efforts for nonwhite educational improvements, but she never instigated these efforts or made them her priority. Thus, indifference more than outright opposition characterized her attitude toward improving education for black students.[77]

Regardless of how much she worked for better teachers, fairer wages, and a sound comprehensive education program, Blanton knew that an unsound financial foundation could literally ruin Texas schools. A successful education program required balanced contributions from state and local sources. She turned then to local support and organized the Better Schools Campaign in 1920. The campaign sought to amend the state constitution so that no local school district was limited in the rate of taxes it could levy for school support. Leading the campaign committee, Blanton put together an array of petitions, parades, songs, letters, and speeches; small tags also were sold to raise money and to offer visible support for the campaign. Modeling the campaign after the recent war drives, the supervisory committee included such influential Texans as Professor Frederick Eby and President Robert Vinson, both of the University of Texas, suffrage activist Jane McCallum, and Baylor University educator Samuel Palmer Brooks. The campaign was an effort to increase both local support, especially in rural areas, and the attention paid to the needs of Texas schools.[78] Blanton was eager to make parents realize that they owed to their children the right of a good education and the opportunity for success in a world whose "future conditions [will be] more complex than those with which you have contended."[79]

People in counties throughout Texas organized support for the amendment, and during the last two weeks in October they waged an intense campaign for education, stressing the need for this permanent solution to school financing as a means to keep the best teachers in Texas (which required paying competitive salaries) and to maintain an opportunity for continued educational improvements. The campaign garnered little opposition and received favorable press coverage, and on November 2, 1920, voters passed the amendment by a 95,000-vote majority and returned an unopposed Blanton for her second two-year term.[80] Despite this victory and a subsequent increase in local school support, one prominent Texas educator noted later that local districts did not take full advantage of the new law and remained too dependent upon the state for school support.[81]

In 1921, Blanton, then serving with Gov. Pat M. Neff, turned to the need for better state funding, arguing that the $14.50 per capita apportionment for schools, a rate that was $7.00 higher than when she had first been elected, was too low. Education expenditures, for Blanton, reflected the state's ideals. Always emphasizing her theme of democracy, she wrote in the *Texas School Journal,* "If we are to retain command of our own institutions and resources, if we are to eliminate the bolshevist, and if we are to cling to the democratic ideals and the high purposes of our forefathers, we must realize that changing conditions have rendered dangerous any future neglect of education."[82] In this endeavor, however, she was less successful than in the Better Schools Campaign, and by January, 1922, the state had lowered the per capita allowance to $13.00. Blanton later maintained that the financial loss had been actually less significant than the fact that she had managed to establish a standard of state support to which a sizeable decrease could not occur without an outcry from the people.[83]

Blanton found herself embroiled in highly political education issues during Neff's tenure as governor. Neff's veto in 1921 of a legislative bill that would have provided four million dollars for rural school aid sent Blanton, working with a variety of women's groups that would soon become known as the Petticoat Lobby, scurrying to have the bill resubmitted in a special legislative session. Educational appropriations became the focus of this session, and Blanton was called upon not only to defend rural aid but also to argue against proposed retrenchment of faculty salaries at higher education facilities, particularly the University of Texas. The results of her efforts were mixed: the fight for rural aid failed, but budget cuts for the University of Texas were less substantial than Blanton and other educational leaders had feared.[84]

Blanton's four years in office provided a continuation of educational programs started before her election, as well as innovative policies that had as their themes democracy, teacher pride, equality for women, and new approaches to the problems of school financing and the need for general educational improvements. However, she was unable to achieve all of her goals. In addition to the reduction of the state's per capita allowance for educational expenditures, the loss of the rural aid appropriation, and the unchanged processes for electing superintendents and paying women teachers, Blanton had to postpone plans for a teachers' retirement fund and an Illiteracy Commission because of lack of support. Still, she successfully merged her particular interests with concrete improvements to Texas schools. She capitalized on the record she inherited and built on her novelty as the first woman state superintendent in Texas. "Because I was the first woman in the office, the people desired to hear me," she later recalled, "and I used this advantage to give them information as to the schools, and to arouse sentiment for educational improvement."[85] In light of her educational accomplishments, it is clear that as state superintendent, Blanton transcended the rhetoric of the 1918 campaign that the suffragists, including herself, had presented, while maintaining the cause of equal rights for women.

Blanton succeeded in many of her endeavors by maintaining a good relationship with both the legislature and governors Hobby and Neff. She also gave credit to a diverse group of supporters who helped her as superintendent: the faithful employees of the Department of Education, most of the members of the legislature, most of the state's teachers, various patriotic societies in Texas, Federated Clubs, Parent-Teachers' Associations, businessmen's luncheon clubs, and the state labor union. Her efforts as superintendent reflected southern Progressive ideals concerning needed school improvements. By raising teacher salaries, lengthening school terms, enforcing compulsory attendance policies, seeking better financial ground, and aiding rural school conditions — and by limiting these efforts primarily to white schools — Blanton acted as did educational reformers throughout the South. The uniqueness of her service lay in her consistent advocacy of the rights of women teachers as part of any reform and her belief that, just as good women voters could cleanse government, so competent women teachers could aid the educational system. Her motivations to increase opportunities for women and to loosen the traditional power of the small group of male educational leaders were related to her belief that, second only to the brewery machine, the teachers' machine was the strongest political organization in Texas. Whether that was indeed true is doubtful; nevertheless, she remained adamant in fighting against it.[86]

Blanton had indicated early in her administration that she would not serve beyond two terms.[87] She was opposed to a long tenure in office because of the possibility that the individual could amass more political power than the office was designed to provide. In addition, she had personal reasons for not remaining in office beyond that time. Even before her first term had ended, she expressed concern over her private financial debt, as well as her own future after leaving office. Her previous interest in running for the U.S. Congress was reinforced by her election in 1918. She hoped to complete her second term and then, if the necessary campaign financing could be raised, to use her office experience to launch a race for the House of Representatives.

Not wavering in her intentions to leave the state superintendent's office after two terms, she cleared the way in 1922 for one of her top assistants, S. M. N. Marrs, to announce for election. Blanton respected Marrs and planned to vote for him, although she pledged to remain publicly neutral in the race when McAllen school superintendent Ed R. Bentley announced against Marrs. However, as the July primary neared, Bentley, a former student of Blanton's at North Texas, attacked Blanton's record, particularly her revision of the teacher certification laws. Clearly annoyed by Bentley's tactics, Blanton lost no time in maneuvering behind-the-scenes in order to warn people of Bentley's background with the teachers' machine, his close relations with some textbook companies, and his probability of fighting with the University of Texas—familiar themes for Blanton to articulate. Marrs won the race in an August runoff, probably because of both Blanton's help and his own strengths. Interestingly, neither Blanton nor Marrs mentioned during the campaign that Bentley was a klansman and was supported by the Ku Klux Klan in his bid.[88]

While Marrs's campaign proceeded, Blanton contemplated the ambitious goal of achieving her own election to Congress. She never considered herself a professional politician; nevertheless, she recognized that her firm convictions and industriousness, as well as the experience and recognition she had gained as superintendent, were political advantages. And she found appealing the opportunity to use these advantages in order to extend her influence on behalf of education. Her victory in 1918, her reelection in 1920, and her general sense of accomplishment while in office led her to believe in 1922 that she could make the run for Congress that she had postponed four years earlier. When the incumbent representative in Denton's thirteenth district, Lucian Parrish, announced that he would resign in order to run for the Senate, Blanton saw what seemed to be the perfect opportunity.[89]

As a woman who understood how important the control of

circumstances could be in politics, and for someone who had
benefited so keenly from timing and successful utilization of political issues in 1918, she must have found the 1922 congressional
race unpredictable and ironic. While Blanton was in Austin de-
bating her final decision to enter the race, other candidates living in the district were already campaigning. She was finally ready
to announce for the July primary when her schedule suddenly
changed. On March 27, 1922, Congressman Parrish died from
injuries sustained in an automobile accident. Blanton then had
to consider running early in a special election in May to fill the
unexpired term, as well as in the July primary for the next full
term. When Parrish's widow indicated that she herself might run
for the unexpired term, Blanton announced that she would not
run against her. But Parrish changed her mind, and on April 5,
Blanton announced that she would enter both races and that she
would remain in state office while doing so by taking some long-
accumulated vacation time prior to the special election.[90]

Blanton planned to conduct a straightforward campaign, emphasizing her service as state superintendent but broadening her
platform to include traditional southern Democratic appeals to
prohibitionists, farmers, and states-righters. She promised to work
for the soldiers' bonus, to reduce the number of federal employees,
and to provide a direct human contact to the national government for her local constituents. She also noted the possible distinction for her district of electing Texas' first congresswoman
and reminded voters that the greatest president in the history
of the United States, Woodrow Wilson, also had been a teacher.
She maintained a feminine approach, affirming in one speech
that, "I know as much about caring for a house and children
as any woman in this room. I do not believe any woman is truly
educated until she has these good womanly accomplishments."
On racial issues, Blanton did come out against the Klan in this
race, but she qualified her opposition by stating that she understood why the group existed and believed that many of its members had worthy motives.[91]

Had the campaign remained on this plateau, Blanton might
have had a better chance to win, even though her opposition was
formidable. As it turned out, she barely had entered the race

before a major debacle occurred concerning her brother, Cong. Thomas L. Blanton of Abilene. The colorful representative, whose career had been characterized by his attacks on labor, communism, and liquor, often alienated his colleagues with his insistence that congressional members spent money too extravagantly and received too many special favors. When he chose, the day after his sister had announced her candidacy, to admonish representatives on the House floor for their selfishness and foolish, petty graft, he succeeded in angering the entire House.[92] The episode embarrassed the Texas delegation and prompted John Nance Garner to say, "Blanton is a discredit to the House and ought to be kicked out."[93]

The brother and sister were close and loyal, if independent from one another in politics, and there is no evidence that he meant to hurt her campaign. That sort of attack was not unusual for him, and he appears simply to have returned to a favorite line of complaint at an inopportune moment. He claimed that the controversy had erupted simply because his colleagues had wanted to use him to hurt his sister's candidacy, though he could not substantiate this accusation. The male-dominated Congress might not have eagerly awaited the arrival of Annie Webb Blanton, but its reaction to her brother appears to have been directed only at him on account of his inflammatory words, which in any case probably had been delivered before many members became aware of his sister's candidacy.[94]

In the midst of this uproar, Annie Blanton proceeded with her campaign, generally upholding her brother but urging voters not to decide for or against her because of his actions. Nevertheless, her brother overshadowed her campaign. He came to Denton late in April to speak on her behalf, but devoted most of his speech to his own defense, hardly even mentioning his sister. Despite her extensive travels throughout the district, the damage was done. On May 13, Blanton finished third in the special election, trailing the winner, state senator Guinn Williams, by more than nine thousand votes. Williams, a wealthy, well-known politician from Decatur, had inherent advantages in the race. Still, Blanton's showing was weak, even where she had expected to be strong: she failed to carry Denton or Denton County. On the day following the election, the *Dallas Morning News* reported on its front page both Williams's election and Tom Blanton's defense of his congressional record.[95]

Her brother's actions surely hurt Blanton's congressional race, but that proved not to be her only weakness. With nationwide full suffrage for women by then a reality, Blanton lacked the specially organized support TESA had provided in 1918. She received some organized female assistance, but her opponents also made appeals to various women's groups in an attempt to divide Blanton's support. Society's general hesitancy to accept a woman for congressional office, a position that held no ties to traditional women's work, also damaged her campaign. In addition, the practical problems of campaigning from Austin against opponents living in the district, and especially against the well-connected Williams, as well as the financial and logistical problems of suddenly facing a special election, further diminished Blanton's chances. In the end, she withdrew from the July primary race and never again ran for a public office.[96]

Yet even in defeat Blanton remained philosophical about her effort and hoped that it had made the way easier for future women candidates. She maintained that women must ever continue to prove their abilities as voters. Looking to the future, she said on the day after the election, "The success of woman suffrage can not be gauged by the success or failure of any one man or woman in any election; it must be measured by whether in the long run, women use the ballot for the good of humanity."[97] The *Dallas Morning News* noted that her good-natured attitude about losing was sure to be noticed by male politicians who had expected a less noble response from a female in the face of political stress and disappointment.[98]

Blanton completed her superintendent's term and spent the remainder of her life in the classroom as an education professor at the University of Texas. Her career as a public official, although not lengthy, proved nonetheless significant. Her election in 1918 and her unsuccessful bid for Congress in 1922 indicate the precarious situation women faced as they fought to obtain the vote and then dealt with the challenge of keeping alive their goals and unity. Blanton had always envisioned more for women than the mere attainment of the right to vote and of breaking into a few isolated roles of political leadership. Still, it was painful for her to discover that one successful election did not necessarily lead to another. Yet she never lost sight of how much competent women could accomplish. "The campaign may bear some fruit in the future even though I lost; for everything that helps to wear away age-old prejudices contributes towards the advancement of women and of humanity," she said in the wake of her loss in 1922.[99] Although acceptance of defeat was difficult for this proud woman, she never indicated regret over any part of her political career. Had she not chosen to run for Congress and not been so determined to serve only two terms as superintendent, she probably could have remained in that office for many years. But she did not question her choices or convictions, and she rarely looked back.

In addition to what it had meant for women, Blanton's public career was significant also for what she had accomplished in education. After a highly charged political campaign that had obliterated the true education issues, she encountered the need to make earlier educational reforms effective in a postwar environment. She confidently rose to the occasion as an officeholder and created her own successful agenda. *Texas School Journal* editor H. T. Musselman, who had been a perceptive and fair critic of Blanton throughout her administration, noted that she had fought bravely for teachers, leaving an important legacy.[100]

Musselman also believed that Blanton's importance would increase with time. Her public career did not create a flood of women officeholders or permanently remove the barriers that women seeking political office would face. No woman after Blanton was ever elected state superintendent in Texas. And into the last decade of the twentieth century, only a few females have followed Blanton into statewide elective office in Texas: Miriam Ferguson, Ann Richards, and Kay Bailey Hutchison, for example. Texas did not send its first woman to Congress until Lera Millard Thomas of Houston was elected in 1966 to replace her deceased husband. These facts, however, do not deny the historical significance of a woman who possessed social vision and political savvy and used her position within a traditionally female profession to bring distinctive feminist leadership, unshakeable conviction, and a Progressive reform spirit to Texas schools, teachers, and women.[101] She left the political arena, having broken some barriers and made some advances, as well as with a personal sense of accomplishment and an eagerness to continue her career as a professional educator.

Education and the University of Texas

1922-40

When the University of Texas created a rural education department in 1927, administrators knew exactly whom they wanted to head this new division in the school of education. She had substantial, unique, and impressive administrative experience, but just as important, she was a veteran of the rural schoolhouse. More recently, she had completed a doctoral degree in rural education from prestigious Cornell University. Annie Webb Blanton happily accepted the challenge, and despite some disappointments it ultimately brought her, this arrangement with the University of Texas allowed her to continue her progressive efforts on behalf of Texas schools and Texas women.

Few precedents existed in 1922 for a woman who sought to reestablish a professional, nonpolitical career after having attained public office. For a strongly motivated and energetic individual like Blanton, the transition had its difficulties. She entered the next phase of her life with no longing to rest on the laurels of her past achievements; her congressional race had satisfied her desire to attempt a bid for higher office. For all practical purposes, she had left politics behind. Blanton expected to remain in the field of education, but after four years in office, she desired also to move beyond her Denton teaching experience and was especially eager to establish herself as an educator *and* a scholar. In retrospect it might appear that employment at the University of Texas was a logical choice as an immediately comfortable and secure job, but closer examination reveals that Blanton spent several years seriously considering other opportunities and that her years at the university, though ultimately fruitful, were not totally comfortable. Nevertheless, her career at Texas, as much as her Denton years and service as state superintendent, proved again that Blanton's energy and ability enabled her to be a fighter and a crusader for education, unwavering in her convictions and unsurpassed in her determination.

As Blanton's second term as state superintendent drew to a close at the end of 1922, two factors heavily influenced the decisions she made regarding her next professional move. First of all, Blanton had invested heavily from her own funds in her 1918 campaign, assuming that the state suffrage organization would be able to help with whatever debt accumulated beyond her personal contributions. That it did not do so is probably attributable to its own restructuring and the organizational challenges it encountered after 1919, as well as to some misunderstood promises and expectations on Blanton's part. Whatever the causes, in 1922 Blanton faced both a large campaign debt and a depleted personal savings account, and she was anxious to undertake a serious effort to reduce her deficit upon leaving office. Blanton did not allow the debt to create a permanent rift between herself and suffrage leaders, but she made no secret of the fact that resolution of the financial burden of the 1918 race had been left to her alone. No doubt this burden also included some expenditures from her 1922 congressional race, but she was more reticent about this debt, which probably was considerably less than that of her previous statewide race. Ultimately, it required more than ten years to clear the balance, even though Blanton had applied to it the proceeds from the sale of her Denton home. As a more direct consequence for her in 1922, the debt created for Blanton a need for immediate employment. She simply could not afford to go unemployed while searching at length for a job best suited to her training, experience, and professional desires.[1]

The second factor concerned Blanton's graduate work. Having studied at both Texas and the University of Chicago for several summers while she had been employed at North Texas, Blanton lacked only a little work to complete her Master's degree in education, which would enhance her career opportunities. Hoping eventually to secure a position in higher education and believing that this probably would take her away from Austin, Blanton sought a path that would allow her to complete her degree promptly and maintain a livable wage. She found such an arrangement by accepting a temporary job working for her successor, S. M. N. Marrs, as the director of the State Board of Examiners. Upon leaving elected office in January, 1923, she began her new duties at an annual salary of thirty-five hundred dollars — only five hundred per year less than she had been paid as state superintendent.[2]

Marrs hired Blanton as a favor to his friend and former boss. The job, offered as hers to keep until she finished her degree, put Blanton in charge of the Board of Examiners Division in the State Department of Education, where she and two additional members supervised the grading of county examinations for teacher certification, maintained permanent records of all current certifications, administered summer normal school examinations for teachers, and directed classification and accreditation of Texas colleges offering certification. Blanton did not find these responsibilities difficult, since she was already familiar with the job's requirements, having overseen them as state superintendent and having watched her close friend Emma Mitchell in the job. Furthermore, Marrs understood that Blanton took the job primarily in order to finish her Master's degree, and he actively encouraged her pursuit of this goal. By March, 1923, she had made arrangements with William Sutton, dean of the University of Texas school of education, to enroll in graduate coursework for the spring term. The energy level that had sustained her as an educator and politician served her once again, as she committed the next several months to her full-time job and full-time studies. "All spring and summer, I put in eight hours a day at the State Department of Education, and another eight on the work for my A.M. degree," she wrote Anna Pennybacker later in the year.[3]

During Blanton's previous studies at Texas, she had worked with Sutton, who had taught in the university's education school since 1897 and had served as its dean since 1909. As state superintendent she had worked with him on routine matters, as well as on a special conference for teachers in 1922. He eagerly supported women in the teaching profession, and Blanton enjoyed a comfortable professional relationship with him. Blanton approached Sutton for assistance with her graduate degree just after he had been asked to serve as acting president of the university, while the regents sought a replacement for Robert E. Vinson, who had resigned in February, 1923. Despite the demands of his new assignment, Sutton promptly advised Blanton as to the necessary paperwork for her graduate program and recommended specific courses and professors.[4]

Blanton concentrated her studies on education, while also pursuing minors in English and Spanish, and she anticipated finishing her Master's degree in the summer of 1923. As she neared the completion of her work, she began to contemplate career opportunities and to consider how and where her services could best be utilized permanently in the field of education. Blanton was eager to attain a position equal to her political and educational experience. She had administered the Texas public schools, had had a lengthy teaching career, and would soon hold a Master's degree in education. She desired a position in higher education, but she was open to other possibilities, if they met her criteria. Whatever position she took, she hoped to utilize her background, be challenged, and continue to advance in her chosen profession. Thus, in June, 1923, she applied to become a statistician for the federal Bureau of Education in Washington, D.C., and asked Sutton to send the Civil Service Commission a letter of recommendation on her behalf. With her application she submitted a copy of her then almost-complete thesis and also gave notice of a forthcoming statistical work she had compiled based on her years in office, to be entitled *A Hand Book of Information as to Education in Texas*. Despite her work and writing, Blanton recognized that her age and gender hindered her chances to be hired; the job description specified that all applicants be under fifty-five years of age and that, though both men and women would be considered, the appointing officers had the right to base their decision on a desired gender.[5] Then almost fifty-three years old, Blanton remained undeterred from making a serious bid for the job, confiding to Sutton that, despite her slim chances, she was applying because she was "desperately in need of a good position."[6]

While Blanton was working on that application, the president of the Texas Federation of Women's Clubs, Lily T. Joseph of San Antonio, contacted Sutton to ask him to help secure a position for Blanton in one of the state's colleges. Sutton let Joseph know that he had just recommended Blanton for the position in the Bureau of Education, but that he would keep her request in mind. The correspondence between Sutton and Joseph reflected Blanton's ongoing interaction with a network of prominent Texas women who were loyal to her, and it also foreshadowed Sutton's later interest in Blanton as a Texas faculty member.[7]

One month later, in July, 1923, Blanton applied for another job, this one an administrative staff position at the newly created, and as yet unlocated, Texas Technological College. In addition to letters of recommendation from leaders in the Texas Federation of Women's Clubs and Superintendent Marrs, Blanton's application was endorsed by Jessie Daniel Ames, then president of the Texas League of Women Voters, which had replaced the Texas Equal Suffrage Association in 1919, and later leader in antilynching and interracial work in the South. In a letter to Amon G. Carter, a regent of the new school, Ames summarized the respect that socially and politically prominent Texas women held for Blanton: "Miss Blanton is very dear to the women who have been working diligently for our public education system. At the end of her ardent four years work as superintendent there is nothing that would be so gratifying to us than to feel that her work had been rewarded by this additional evidence of approval. I do not exaggerate when I say that if this selection could be left to the popular vote of the women, Miss Blanton would be unanimously elected."[8]

At the same time that she applied for this position, Blanton submitted her Master's thesis, "A Study of Educational Progress in Texas, 1918–1922," to the University of Texas. The project measured the progress of education in each Texas county based on ten standards, including high school enrollment percentages, teachers' preparation, teachers' salaries, and local taxation for educational purposes. Her work concluded that Texas schools still needed improvements but that "the state of Texas, has during the last four years, made more rapid progress in educational efficiency than any other period of equal length in the past."[9] Consistent with her ideas on minority education, it also noted that the overall poor showing of East Texas in her study could be attributed to the heavy burden that region carried in educating black students.[10]

The thesis was more than three hundred pages, and her submission of it only a few months after returning to graduate school indicates its heavy reliance on information compiled while she had been in office. The university's generosity in accepting this project, largely done prior to her enrollment and which lauded her own achievements, is apparent. However, the thesis did provide a detailed and interesting historical record of education in Texas for the four years that she directed the state's schools, and the university considered Blanton's professional work as the top administrator of the Texas public school system to contribute appropriately to her degree.

As the summer of 1923 wore on, Blanton's degree was all but officially awarded, and still she had no indication that she would be hired by either the Bureau of Education or Texas Tech. At this point acting university president Sutton, aware of her situation and respecting her accomplishments, approached Blanton about the possibility of a position at Texas that might provide a satisfactory arrangement for her, even if it was not long-term. Blanton was interested, since she had no other acceptable offers for positions.[11] On August 9, 1923, she wrote to Sutton that she hoped he would remain as president of the university, "both because I want you there and because your plan for me can be carried out." She added that she hoped he would contact her soon since she was in some suspense about her future. She did not have to wait long. By August 20, she knew her appointment at the university was certain. Blanton received her Master's degree on August 31, completed her work with the state board on September 20, and on September 21, 1923, began as adjunct professor in the educational administration department of the school of education at the University of Texas.[12]

Her job search had not quite reached the point of desperation, but it had come closer to it than an accomplished and proud woman such as Blanton would have preferred. Thus her new job, though only part-time and offering a salary of only twenty-six hundred dollars a year, was pleasing; it was a position in higher education of which she could be proud, and it solved her immediate need for employment.[13] "I like my new work very much, and every one is very kind and considerate of me," she wrote to Pennybacker in October. With her pride intact, she boasted to Pennybacker that "the position was offered to me without solicitation on my part, and I have had many lovely letters from various parts of the state, in which friends have expressed gratification at my appointment." Her friends also expressed their pleasure to others. Her appointment prompted Lily Joseph to write to Sutton, "I feel that I am warranted in the statement that the women throughout Texas will rejoice in the recognition that you have given her." H. T. Musselman noted in the *Texas School Journal* that, although Blanton had considered other jobs for "pleasure and profit," he always believed that the gods had intended for her to teach and was happy to report her enthusiasm at returning to the classroom to train future teachers.[14]

Blanton herself was pleased that the university wanted her and that her new colleagues, many of whom she already knew from her educational work in the state, seemed genuinely glad to work with her. Although she did not expect the job to be longstanding, as it eventually became, she believed in 1923 that it could lead to other appropriate career choices, an important factor for a woman of dignity. Her loyalty to the university as an alumna, as well as her respect and appreciation for Sutton, contributed to her eagerness to begin her new opportunity.[15]

The university's school of education began in 1891 as a school of pedagogy devoted to preparing students to teach at secondary and college levels, leaving elementary preparation to the state's normal school in Huntsville. By 1920, following several name changes and internal restructuring, the school of education emerged with approximately fifteen faculty members organized into four divisions: art of teaching (chaired by J. L. Henderson), educational administration (chaired by B. F. Pittenger), history of education (chaired by Frederick Eby), and philosophy of education (chaired by Alexander Caswell Ellis). As dean of the school since 1909, Sutton had supervised, in addition to organizational changes, an increase in the number of faculty and students, the beginning of a practice teacher program in conjunction with the Austin public schools, and a relocation of the school from the university's main building to a nearby new three-story structure. At the time that Blanton joined its faculty in 1923, the school had more than twelve hundred students enrolled in its classes, three-quarters of them female. The school offered a bachelor of science degree, although many of the students in education classes enrolled in other programs. Graduate courses in the education school led only to a Master's degree until 1934, when a Doctor of Education degree program was added. Nevertheless, when the school hired Blanton in 1923, it was already large enough to provide comprehensive teacher training while offering the benefits of a full-fledged university. Unlike her experience at North Texas, Blanton's teaching now was in the context of true higher education. She began her first year by teaching courses in school organization and management as well as a graduate seminar on educational administration.[16]

Immediately upon assuming her position at Texas, Blanton had the opportunity to witness firsthand how one of her reforms as state superintendent was being carried out. While in office, she had consulted representatives from various teacher training programs in Texas prior to initiating an effort in 1921 to raise teacher certification standards. After these consultations, Blanton proposed a new law that included a requirement that a minimum number of college education courses, including observation and student teaching, be taken before a first-class certificate could be awarded. Part of the law's provisions, perceived, and consequently opposed, by some normal schools as unnecessary state intrusion into their own domain, had gone into effect before Blanton left office, with full enactment to occur by 1925. Larger schools such as the University of Texas, which were less threatened by the law's provisions than normal schools and better able to incorporate them, viewed the reform as a needed improvement in teacher training, and Blanton found the opportunity to be directly involved in these newly required courses especially gratifying.[17]

By the fall of 1923, Blanton still had not realized she had found her permanent professional home at Texas. It was almost two years later before she felt fully confident that the university considered her a long-term investment and would allow and encourage her to pursue the additional studies, scholarly writing, and appropriate career advancements that she desired.[18] Her hesitancy to look upon her employment at Texas as permanent related in large part to her uncertainty about the university's future leader. Blanton had secured her position because of Sutton, whose own role as acting president was to end in July, 1924. Although Sutton remained as dean of education for several years after that, and was active in university affairs until his death in 1928, Blanton realized that it would be difficult for Sutton to retain her, a recently hired, part-time employee, if a new president would wish otherwise. Futhermore, she had enough experience to recognize that the university president had many constituencies to please and that powerful people could apply pressure to cut budgets and reduce staff in one area in order to benefit another. If the new president perceived that she held her position as a favor from Sutton, she feared the consequences. Some twenty years and four university presidents later, when she retired, such fears were shown to have been unfounded, but in 1923 they were quite real to her.[19]

These concerns, as well as the desire for full-time work, led Blanton again to confront the job market toward the end of her first year of teaching at the university. She had been pleasantly surprised in the spring of 1924, when the club women of Houston, including representatives of the League of Women Voters, Council of Jewish Women, and Child Welfare League, had endorsed and nominated her as a candidate for superintendent of the Houston schools. She reported this development to Sutton in March, indicating that although she had not been selected, she had been honored by the effort. Three months later, she let Sutton know that she believed she had a fair chance to be hired at Texas Tech, which was by then being established at Lubbock, as the head of the English or education department.[20] She actually preferred to remain at Texas, as she wrote Sutton, but felt obliged to consider that position: "If conditions in the future should be such that I can continue to work in the University with the feeling that I am wanted and valued, and that opportunities of advancement are open to me as I may earn them and deserve them, I should prefer to remain in the University. I love the University, opportunities for study and improvement are better here than I should have in West Texas, and, what is very important to me, my best beloved sister [May] lives in Austin. I should prefer to teach on a smaller salary and be near her, than to take a more lucrative position in West Texas." Blanton concluded that if she had to leave, the work at a new school would be appealing, but that she would accept no offer from Tech's president Paul Horn without consulting first with Sutton. She also expressed to Sutton her appreciation for his encouragement and assistance in planning her future doctoral work, indicating that a desire to continue her graduate studies also influenced her considerations.[21]

Then fifty-three years of age, Blanton was concentrating completely on establishing herself as a permanent and fully credentialed university faculty member. She recognized the worthiness and satisfaction of teaching and administrative work, which were well-represented on her résumé, but she was also eager to broaden her educational experience by earning her credentials as a scholar and, thus, to improve her own opportunities in higher education. Such a goal was not unheard of for a woman at this time, but it was rare, and Blanton knew she would have to be persistent if she were to achieve her goals. In the years that Blanton was employed at Texas, women comprised between 20 and 30 percent of the faculty at public four-year colleges and universities in the United States. Percentages at Texas approximated this range, and Blanton gained encouragement from female colleagues who held or were pursuing advanced graduate degrees. Still, only about 15 percent of the doctorates awarded in the nation went to women at the time that Blanton earned hers, and many women scholars of the era believed that holding advanced degrees only served to increase discrimination against them, with the benefits of pursuing such degrees being more intrinsic than rewarding in terms of rank or salary. Blanton determined to receive her doctorate, and she never expressed, before or after earning the degree, any discouragement about that pursuit. She was, however, realistically aware of the dedication demanded by such an effort and thus attempted it with her usual, intense determination.[22]

Blanton apparently received no offer from President Horn at Tech, but Texas rehired her as adjunct professor for the 1924–25 school year with no change in salary. The year began with a new university president, Walter M. Splawn, a former economics professor at the university and chair of the Texas Railroad Commission. Blanton and Splawn ultimately developed a friendly working relationship, and he took an active interest in her doctoral work in 1926. But in the fall of 1924 one final offer tempted Blanton to leave the university. Despite her indications to Sutton that she preferred Austin and the university, another place in Texas held a hometown appeal for her, and when the presidency of the College of Industrial Arts (CIA) was vacated in Denton in September, 1924, Blanton applied for the position. This application strictly was based on personal appeal; her position at Texas was secure for at least another year, so she was not desperate for new employment. But the chance to run a college for women, in a town where she had lived for seventeen years, was exciting and offered challenges few other positions could rival.

Letters of recommendation from professionally prominent friends and colleagues supported her application as usual, but by mid-October the school's board had selected Lindsey Blayney as its new president. Blanton confided to her longtime friend Anna Pennybacker, who had written a letter of support for her, that apparently she and Dr. Blayney had been the two main contenders for the job but that, according to CIA board member and Blanton supporter Lily Joseph, a majority of the board refused to give serious consideration to hiring a woman. She directed her disappointment at unspecified female members of the college's board, writing to Pennybacker, "I fear that we have to accept the fact that while the people will elect women to executive positions, women, generally, when they are board members, will not support one of their own sex for such places." She then added dryly, "I'm glad I can always see the funny side of things."[23]

The experience made a strong impression on Blanton, and when in June, 1926, Blayney was fired because of his poor administrative skills, she let Lily Joseph know that she would apply again only if CIA would seriously consider a woman for the presidency. Otherwise, she recommended University of Texas Dean of Students Louis Hubbard for the job. Joseph acknowledged that the school would not hire a woman, and she and Blanton then encouraged Hubbard, who was indeed selected as the new president. [24]

Blanton's pursuit of other job opportunities ceased after her CIA experience. She did, however, allow friends to organize a letter-writing campaign to president-elect Franklin Roosevelt in 1933, which recommended her as U.S. Commissioner of Education. Molly Dewson, as head of the Women's Division of the Democratic National Committee, was busy at this time working to bring women into New Deal positions, and a prominent group of Texas educators and Blanton supporters saw a unique opportunity to attain a national office for the university professor. However, perhaps because she feared the embarrassment of rejection, Blanton asked that her friends go about their campaign as quietly as possible, and in the end, she did not get the job. [25] Her experiences after leaving the superintendent's office indicate that despite having been Texas' first woman elected to statewide office and its highest education official, Blanton still faced many barriers as a female professional. Most administrative jobs in higher education were reserved for males, and even Blanton did not succeed at ending that tradition. It is indicative of her suspicions of irresolute women that she blamed female board members for worsening this situation. It also suggests that while Blanton expected to encounter discrimination from some males, she was annoyed by any woman who did not recognize her abilities and prove loyal to her. Since her days of working for suffrage, Blanton's feminism and Progressivism had allowed her to see the potential of certain women to make positive contributions to society as citizens, voters, professionals, and decision makers. But when women failed to live up to this potential or to recognize it in other women, she was extremely disappointed.

Despite these experiences, Blanton avoided any lasting bitterness, and she proceeded to capitalize on the opportunity the university provided. Her adjunct status continued for a third year in 1925–26, but by 1925 Blanton saw that her position at the university had greater potential, and she found a way to enhance her professional opportunities there.

From her first teaching experience in Pine Springs, Blanton had taken an interest in rural education. As state superintendent, she continued this interest and took pride in creating some constructive changes in this seriously deficient aspect of Texas education. Upon joining the Texas faculty, and especially after her first year, Blanton began to advocate the need for the university to develop further its training in rural education and to have a faculty specialist in that field. Sutton agreed with her assessment, and by 1925 Pittenger, who was not only the chair of the educational administration department but also Sutton's closest assistant and future successor as dean, had come to agree as well. In June of that year, Pittenger informed University President Splawn that he had offered to start a rural education department in the school of education and to put Blanton in charge of it, contingent upon her completion of a doctorate in rural education. The degree, for which she was already taking some classes at the university, could be completed at Texas if she wished, and her new duties would result in her promotion to associate professor, with opportunities for further advancements. [26]

This arrangement marked the beginning of a confident, trusting, and fruitful long-term relationship between Blanton and the University of Texas. The opportunity to earn her doctorate, and then to take up the challenge of organizing an academic department in order to help solve some critical educational problems, excited Blanton, and she believed the task worthy of her abilities. For university officials, the situation presented an opportunity to retain an alumna and a valued teacher, while moving the school into the forefront of rural education training.

Blanton did not have to exaggerate the problems of one-teacher and county schools; statistics showed that such schools suffered — far beyond their urban counterparts — short terms, poor teacher salaries, limited funding, and undertrained teachers. [27] The *Texas School Journal* had noted in 1922 that Texas paid too much attention to urban school improvements at the expense of rural needs, "which simply shows that Texas knows how to take care of her favored few but has not yet chiseled out some plan to take care of her unfavored many." As a large state with a nonurban population of almost 70 percent in the early 1920s, Texas faced serious, pervasive rural education problems. By dealing with these problems in an academic setting and preparing future educators specifically for teaching in this field, Blanton knew she could address directly what she considered to be Texas' most pressing educational need. To longtime advocates of educational reform in Texas, such as Sutton, Blanton's ideas appeared sound. There were other educational problems in the state equally serious — the education of minorities, for example — but as her earlier career had demonstrated, Blanton had neither the interest nor the experience to commit to them as she did to rural education. She gave the progress and needs of county schools and rural education careful and detailed accounting in her 1922 educational handbook; in contrast, regarding progress for non-white educational facilities, she wrote simply that "schools for negroes and Mexicans have been greatly improved" without offering details. Thus efforts in rural education at the university reflected her earlier interests and priorities.[28]

As Blanton continued her teaching and graduate work at the university for the 1925–26 school year, she determined that her own doctoral degree in rural education should be attained elsewhere in order to give her the extensive background of scholarship and training that would be necessary for her future work at Texas. Consequently, she applied for a leave of absence from Texas for 1926–27 to study at Cornell University in Ithaca, New York. With the administrative assistance of Splawn, a fifteen-hundred-dollar scholarship from the General Education Board in New York City, and five hundred dollars from the university, she began her studies at Cornell in July, 1926.[29]

In the 1920s, Cornell was a leading school for rural education training, maintaining a faculty of twelve specialists in this field. Texas educators were familiar with the school beyond its reputation because one of Cornell's rural education professors, George A. Works, had lived temporarily in Texas to direct the statewide survey of public education carried out under Governor Neff in 1924. Works proved a valuable advisor to Blanton in Ithaca, suggesting that she fulfill the requirements that Pittenger had recommended for her doctoral work by taking both rural education and rural sociology courses. Works and Professor Clyde B. Moore served on her major field committee in rural education, with Professor R. M. Stewart directing her first minor in school administration, and Professor Bruce L. Melvin covering her second minor in rural social organization.[30]

Throughout her year in New York, Blanton maintained close contact with Splawn and her university colleagues. Splawn had suggested to Blanton before she left Austin that she might benefit from taking some classes also at Columbia University in New York City. Blanton considered this possibility but decided that Columbia's rural education curriculum and the quality of the faculty did not justify the additional effort. Had she studied at Columbia, her work would have been done under two female professors, but that did not ease her concerns about the overall quality of the program. Not desiring to study under professors she perceived as less competent, Blanton dutifully confirmed her assessment and decision with Splawn but diplomatically added that Columbia might possibly be a place for her to do future work, "as I shall always wish to study every two or three years." Splawn expressed confidence in her decision, but Blanton never attended Columbia.[31]

Blanton spent just over a year at Cornell, taking courses, studying German, and researching and writing her dissertation. To save money on rent, she lived in one of Cornell's university houses as chaperon to eighteen female students. She conducted her research in both Ithaca and Washington, D.C., where she worked in the Library of Congress and the Bureau of Education. From her correspondence with friends and colleagues in Austin, it appears that she devoted her year almost exclusively to schoolwork; she pushed to finish her dissertation in time for a defense before classes resumed at Texas in late September, 1927. The pressure she felt to complete her work manifested itself in one of her last letters from Ithaca to Pittenger, shortly before she took her oral examinations over her coursework and dissertation. "Please don't be disappointed in me if I should fail on the examination," she wrote. "I'm frightfully nervous about it.

I'd hate to disgrace the University of Texas in that way, so I'll do my best."[32]

Cornell University officially awarded Blanton the doctor of philosophy degree on September 28, 1927, following acceptance of her dissertation, "A Study of the County as a Factor in the Development of School Control." The work, a complex study, first examined the development of county control of schools in six states, including Texas, and then compared this control with trends in a second group of six states. Her research included analysis of general statutes, school laws, educational reports, and histories for her twelve selected states. The study did not seek to pass judgment on the overall efficiency of county school administration, but rather to explain why and how county administration had developed and evolved. In contrast to her Master's thesis, the dissertation required extensive new research for Blanton, and its completion in one year was indeed a major accomplishment.[33]

Blanton returned to Texas in the fall of 1927 and was immediately promoted to associate professor and chair of the new rural education department at an annual salary of thirty-six hundred dollars. For the next thirteen years, Blanton devoted herself to teaching and scholarship, and her rank and seniority in the school of education steadily rose. In 1933 she became a full professor, and as only the third woman in the university's history to attain this position, she was extremely proud of the promotion. Indicating her emphasis on scholarly pursuits, she noted later that "the two greatest distinctions I ever received, in my opinion, were being elected to Phi Beta Kappa, and being made a full professor in the University of Texas."[34]

Blanton maintained cordial yet candid relationships with her subsequent bosses, who in addition to Dean Pittenger included university presidents H. Y. Benedict (1927–37), J. W. Calhoun (1937–39), and Homer P. Rainey (1939–44). As her seniority increased, her willingness to speak out for faculty concerns also grew. In 1935, she tactfully explained to President Benedict, the former dean of the university's college of arts and sciences, that most faculty members found it difficult to meet the deadline for insurance premiums because it coincided with the due date for city taxes, and she suggested instead a ninety-day, staggered-payment plan. Benedict did not have the legal authority to establish the ninety-day plan, but he promised Blanton that he would investigate the possibility of moving the deadline to a different season.[35] Such an exchange indicates not only the direct and rather informal relationship between faculty and administrators that flourished at the university earlier in this century, but also Blanton's candid nature, the security she felt in her position, and her confidence in the university to deal in good faith with its faculty.

Despite her own rise in rank, Blanton found the establishment of rural education as a permanent department in the school of education to be difficult. In the fall of 1927, she returned to the university excited about the creation of the new department, although the university's budget provided for her alone as a rural education faculty member for 1927–28. She initially offered only two courses: one on the basics of rural education and one on rural school administration. Still, the number of students enrolled in her five classes pleased Blanton, who believed that it indicated the university's potential to become a regional leader in rural education, just like Cornell. To aid in the promotion of her program she helped to organize a Conference on Rural Problems in the summer of 1928, held at the university and sponsored by the university's division of extension. Blanton reported that the conference had drawn educators from across the state and that it might become an annual event. She also began making tentative plans to establish an arrangement with a rural school in Travis County to allow practice and observation by future teachers. Her plan for rural education at the university focused on expansion, and she knew the success of the program would depend on increasing faculty positions and student enrollment.[36]

Behind this optimism, however, Blanton realized that even with the university's support, the rural education program needed more financial assistance than the legislature was providing. She understood that a small program could be considered expendable by lawmakers, and she wanted not only to avoid this possibility but also to increase her department's budget in order to accomplish the goals she had. Thus in January, 1929, when the rural education program was less than two years old, Blanton wrote Bene-

dict and suggested that she begin to make "quiet efforts" to secure an endowment for a rural education chair at the university.
She planned to find a wealthy Texan—she apparently had no specific person in mind—to donate the money and, thus, to allow
the rural program to expand quickly and accomplish within a
few years what otherwise might take much longer. Blanton admitted to Benedict that her idea might be too visionary and prove
futile, but she saw no harm in attempting it. Benedict agreed.

The next two months, however, brought only more setbacks.
Blanton continued her personal campaign for rural education,
seeking funding and also conducting her own research on one-
teacher schools and on the use of rural schools as social centers,
but her support network was dwindling. The second statewide
conference on rural education that Blanton had hoped might
become an annual affair was cancelled because of a lack of funds.
Not only did increased state funding for her department appear
doomed, but a complete elimination of her budget for the following year seemed likely. Consequently, she turned to the General
Education Board in New York to request either financial assistance for the continuation of her department for a limited time
or endowment of the rural education chair. Blanton explained
to Benedict that she thought her chances with the board were
good because it had previously given her a scholarship for her
rural education doctoral work and because, as state superintendent, she had cooperated with the board on educational matters
pertaining to blacks at a time when few other school leaders in
Texas were participating in such endeavors. In addition to this
effort for funding, Blanton also organized a program to raise
money for university scholarships to allow rural teachers to take
special training classes.[37]

Ultimately, none of Blanton's plans for the rural education department came to fruition, and in the fall of 1929 she was moved
back to the educational administration department, where she
continued to teach rural education as well as other administrative classes. Her interest in and advocacy of rural education as
both a social problem and academic discipline continued until
her death. It was during these years in the late 1920s, however,
when she developed her strongest scholarly convictions on the

issue, and her activities of this time provide some insight into the academic personality of Blanton.

After 1927, Blanton's own future at the university was secure, so her ongoing efforts on behalf of rural education arose from a genuine interest and response to challenge rather than as a personal job-saving crusade. She was willing to work largely on her own to establish and fund the new department because she understood that to be her job as head of the department (and its only faculty member). She kept President Benedict and Dean Pittenger informed of developments and occasionally asked for their assistance, such as providing additional letters to potential funders. But she was realistic enough not to expect them simply to create money for her department when the legislature did not provide it. She was energetic and independent enough to seek such money on her own, rather than accept the legislature's allotment as the department's absolute destiny. The continuation of the rural education department in 1929 required either ample outside funding or incredible legislative lobbying. The former, Blanton sought but could not find; the latter, she had neither interest nor authorization to pursue. She knew that her colleagues agreed with her argument for the need for rural education at that time, and that was all she expected from them. Having been state superintendent, Blanton had some insight into state appropriations, and she realized that without much larger enrollment figures to justify her monetary requests, lawmakers would not provide adequate funding for starting and developing the program of which she dreamed. She avoided criticizing specific members of the legislature, but her experience with legislators led her to confide to Benedict that "many of our problems of rural education are precisely those about which members of the legislature entertain the strongest prejudices."[38]

The goals that Blanton dreamed of were ambitious, and she seems to have had no shortage of ideas for how a program of rural education could be developed at the university. Blanton coupled these idealistic visions with a practical, hard-working spirit, and although her dreams for the department failed, she never regretted her efforts or felt bitterness over these events. Nine years after her permanent move back to the educational admin-

istration department, Pittenger sought her input on rural education needs. Blanton responded with suggestions very similar to
those she had made in the late 1920s: the need to endow a chair
for rural education, to find funds to establish a practice school,
and to hold an annual conference on rural life and education.
She reminded Pittenger that it was the university which should
take the lead in the study of rural problems and the training of
rural teachers and administrators, since the only other college
offering such training in Texas was the Agricultural and Mechanical College, where the focus was on agriculture and home economics and where many teachers would never be comfortable
in its military school environment and women were not even admitted. She also noted that until the university added rural education classes to the required curriculum for education students,
their enrollment numbers would remain lower than for courses
that students had to take to graduate. She understood that difficulties existed in establishing a separate rural education department but remained convinced that such a department could serve
a valid purpose at the university and give rural education an opportunity to expand as an academic discipline.[39]

Blanton's rural education concerns dominated her academic
work at the university, but her publication record during this
time covered other specializations as well. Because Blanton had
published textbooks prior to her employment at Texas, it is not
surprising that she maintained ongoing research and writing projects after joining the university faculty. She had completed *A Hand
Book of Information as to Education in Texas, 1918–1922* soon after leaving the state superintendent's office, and it was published by the
State Department of Education in 1923. Her concept for the book
had derived from inquiries the department had received while
Blanton was state superintendent and from her belief that a standard education handbook could provide needed information to
the public. In it she addressed teachers' salaries and contracts,
rural education, recognition of female educators, and assimila-
tion of foreigners, and through it, along with her thesis, she provided ample written documentation of the status of education
in Texas during her years in office.

In 1928 she once again turned her interests to the subject of grammar and published, through the Southern Publishing Company in Dallas, *Advanced English Grammar*. This book, intended as a high school text, was adopted by schools in Texas, Tennessee, Kentucky, and Georgia and was praised for its practical and thorough approach to grammar. Blanton had begun this five hundred–page work many years earlier and apparently found enough time to complete it during her hectic year of doctoral studies in New York. She expressed her appreciation for professional help over the years by dedicating the book to her "esteemed friend and former teacher" William Sutton. *Advanced English Grammar* further enhanced Blanton's reputation as a grammar specialist; even into the late 1980s it was referred to as an exemplary text.[40]

Understandably, though, Blanton's primary scholarly research and writing projects focused on rural education. The most ambitious publication effort Blanton undertook as a university faculty member was her study of one-teacher schools. She began this research under the auspices of the American Association of University Women (AAUW) in 1928. The AAUW had emerged in 1921 from the Association of Collegiate Alumnae and offered organizational comradery and study of education problems for white women scholars and teachers at all levels. In the 1920s its growth across the country made it a major national women's organization, and in Texas an active membership flourished and included many of the female faculty members in Austin.[41]

As chair of the Texas Division's Rural Education Committee for AAUW, Blanton directed plans for a proposed one-teacher school study designed to compare urban and rural schools based on a detailed sampling of students in both types of facilities throughout the state. Blanton, typically displaying devotion to her cause, prepared lengthy background reports on rural education for AAUW members and then encouraged them to offer a patriotic service to Texas by studying and solving the problems of rural education. Her goal was to conduct her study of one-teacher schools on a statewide basis and at the same time to encourage AAUW members to study their own local rural schools. The combined effect was designed to enable AAUW, with direction from Blanton's committee, to undertake a crucial role in attaining specific rural education improvements, such as better training for rural teachers, more state funding for poorer districts, and a lowering of the beginning school age from seven to six to ensure more schooling for rural students, who often dropped out at age fourteen, the age at which school attendance was no longer mandatory. Her work with AAUW both complemented her university efforts and softened her personal disappointment caused by the funding difficulties in the rural education department at Texas. Blanton's writings about this project make clear her motivations at the university: she believed Texas' overall educational standing was held down by inferior rural schools and that the existing discrepancies between rural and urban educational opportunities were inherently undemocratic.[42] She expressed her disdain for this situation in one AAUW correspondence: "There is nothing to hold us in the lowest rank except ignorance of what constitutes a good school system, adherence to inefficient methods of the past, and the efforts of ultra conservative politicians, some of whom have private axes to grind."[43] For Blanton, improvements to rural education reflected a Progressive effort to raise Texas' standards for education and were related to other school reforms that she had advocated since her Denton days. She recognized that some people still equated rural concerns strictly with the sympathies of Jim Ferguson, but she resolved to remove rural education from this partisan arena.

In 1930, Blanton submitted her plan for a study of one-teacher schools to the Laura Spellman Rockefeller Fund for Research in the Social Sciences, which subsequently agreed to provide, through the university, money for testing students, for Blanton's travels, and for one semester of her salary, thus enabling her to take a leave of absence from Texas in the spring of 1931 to carry out her research.[44] Even for the energetic Blanton, it was to be a major task, as she later noted: "The semester's leave of absence was utilized in the actual giving of tests, but the rating of tests, compilation of grades, formulation of tables, and similar activities, have been pursued in such time as a busy University teacher, carrying on full-time class work, can snatch from other engulfing demands."[45] Blanton had hoped that the results of her study, when prepared in written form, would be the most extensive study available comparing urban and rural schools in the United States.

However, time and monetary limitations ultimately narrowed her work in scope, and she focused on only three Texas counties rather than a broader range of the state.[46]

The university's Bureau of Research in the Social Sciences published Blanton's study in 1936 as *The Child of the Texas One-Teacher School.* Her statistics on urban and one-teacher schools, based on standardized tests given in one-teacher schools and then compared with existing data on urban schools, included comparisons of basic skills in areas such as reading, handwriting, and math, as well as indications of social and economic differences. Blanton compiled her evidence from a total of eight schools in Travis, Nacogdoches, and Ellis counties, but she remained convinced, with some justification, that this limited sample truly represented a major enlargement in the field of comparative urban-rural studies. Her selected schools included no black facilities, but the study did measure separate results on forty Spanish-speaking students. Maintaining her tendency to make racial judgments and reflecting her own biases, she carefully noted that most of the nonwhite students in her study were of Spanish rather than Mexican descent.[47]

Despite its narrowly based and racially discriminatory sampling, Blanton's study did in fact represent a sound methodology because it was based on actual visits to rural Texas schools to measure students' specific mental, physical, and social skills. Her conclusions about the generally inferior status of rural students were not surprising, but Blanton demonstrated how environment and daily life affected students' schoolwork, how male and female students differed in individual performances, and how society needed to alleviate the discrepancies between the overall qualities of life in rural and urban areas. She avoided in her analysis any tone of condescension toward rural students and reflected her serious and sincere concern for improving rural education in Texas.[48]

Blanton did not resolve the problems in rural education. However, her studies, teachings, and extracurricular efforts in this matter resulted in an increased awareness of those problems and ultimately led to some gradual improvements. Among the many Texas educators concerned with rural education, Blanton approached it the most clearly as a Progressive reform, and no one did more for rural education in Texas in the first half of the twentieth century than she.

Through her research, publishing, and administrative efforts with rural education, Blanton devoted herself to a career of scholarly achievement during her years at the university. She also served, as required, on various university committees and fulfilled other extracurricular duties. Despite these diverse and time-consuming activities, her role in the classroom and emphasis on teaching did not diminish. Blanton was known for possessing a natural ability to teach, although her presentations were more practical than entertaining. She imparted her deep-rooted concern for rural education not only through class lectures, but also on numerous field trips to one-teacher schools throughout Travis County. She had a reputation as a friendly and caring professor and was respected for her knowledge on educational matters, although many of her students remained unaware of her specific history as a Texas educator. In her courses, she did not discuss her previous political activities or her firsthand experiences as state superintendent. She considered her classroom a place to impart knowledge on school administration and rural education, and she saw no need to color this serious task with self-indulgent reminiscences. This stance also reflected her tendency to devote herself to the present with no desire to rest upon past accomplishments. Dean Pittenger later recalled that despite her lengthy administrative experience and his relative inexperience as a dean, she never intruded in university affairs unless her assistance was requested.[49]

Those who interacted with Blanton during this time remember a woman who was well-known on campus and maintained congenial relationships with students and colleagues alike. She could be demanding—at times even somewhat of a perfectionist—and she projected a rather serious, yet unobtrusive, image as a woman driven to accomplish specific goals and tasks. Her stocky frame was always properly, if not elegantly, attired, and former students recall her as a captivating feminine presence, although she claimed no striking physical attributes. She reserved the full dimensions

of her personality for her closest friends, usually through connections with Delta Kappa Gamma, the professional women
teacher's society with which she had been affiliated since having
founded it in 1929.[50]

Blanton's full-time employment with the University of Texas
ended in the spring of 1940, when her impending seventieth birthday mandated, according to Texas law, a reduction to modified
service. Blanton felt no need to retire and would have preferred
to remain a full-time employee, but having no choice in the matter, she met with Pres. Homer P. Rainey to arrange her move
to modified service. She used this opportunity to remind Rainey
of the ongoing needs in rural education, despite some recent decline in interest in it at the university, and encouraged him to
study some information she had gathered on the topic. Concerning her personal situation, Blanton was less animated. She asked
Rainey not to publicize her retirement and let him know that
her part-time university salary would be supplemented with a
salary she would draw for work with Delta Kappa Gamma.
Modified service meant teaching only one course per semester,
but with the help of Fred Ayer, who then chaired the educational
administration department, Blanton was allowed to teach a second course because of both her "peculiar fitness" and the department's needs. Ayer, a longtime colleague of Blanton's, also welcomed her continued use of the department as a base for her
various educational endeavors. In July, 1940, regent Lutcher Stark
wrote a letter to Ayer, requesting that every consideration be given
to benefit from Blanton's talents as she entered this phase with
the university. All in all, her transition to modified service occurred quietly, as she had wished. She preferred as little change
as possible in her university position, and for the five remaining
years of her life, until just a few months before her death, she
approached her job with no less vigor or enthusiasm.[51]

From 1923 to 1940 Blanton had progressed at the university
from an uncertain adjunct professor to a confident, established,
and scholarly senior professor. During these years, she consistently approached her position as if just beginning her career.
She proved herself worthy of a permanent teaching job by obtaining graduate degrees, fighting for rural education, actively

pursuing research and publishing projects, and refusing to enter a classroom without thorough preparation. She began at Texas when she was past her fiftieth birthday, after she had gained rare firsthand political experience and an extensive knowledge of Texas schools. Her work at the university proved that she desired to fight for new accomplishments and to face new challenges at every stage of her life, and that she could do this with a consistently focused, intense devotion to her cause.

Blanton benefited from the university's period of general growth and positive changes during her employment. When she joined the university's faculty in 1923, there were approximately nine thousand students and three hundred faculty members. At the time of her move to modified service in 1940, there were more than eleven thousand students in Austin and five hundred faculty members. The years produced no major political upheavals until the presidency of Homer Rainey, a sympathetic New Dealer who tangled with the more conservative board of regents. Because Rainey's dismissal in November, 1944, came just a few months before Blanton's retirement and death in 1945, she was only marginally involved in this controversy. Most of Blanton's university employment had coincided with the years of relative tranquility between the Ferguson fight of 1917 and the Rainey episode, and thus no major political battles affected her service.[52]

During her years at the university, Blanton's professional endeavors often involved interaction with males in higher positions of authority. Judging from her communications with these men and her career advancement at Texas, this situation proved not to be a problem. Not all of Blanton's energies went directly to professional endeavors, however, and when she pursued activities away from the classroom, she maintained her preference for the company of other women. She shared a home near the university for several years with her friend Cora Martin, a member of the elementary education faculty, before moving to the University Faculty Women's Club, where she lived comfortably with colleagues such as Martin, Dean of Women Ruby Terrill, and education faculty member Clara Parker. The university's small community of female faculty members — around seventy-five to one hundred women throughout Blanton's service — were close and shared similar backgrounds in educational preparation, teaching experiences, and extracurricular activities. To judge by her work with Delta Kappa Gamma, this element of university life greatly influenced Blanton.[53]

Family concerns were also a significant factor in Blanton's private life after she joined the university faculty. In 1934, after eleven years of university teaching, Blanton's financial situation had improved sufficiently to allow her to purchase her own home on Cliff Street in Austin. Unlike her home in Denton, she shared this residence only with her family. After her older sister May, for whom she always maintained a deep affection and appreciation, was seriously injured in a fire and subsequently bedridden, Blanton invited her and her husband Frank Hill to move from their country home just outside Austin and to join her in town. Their daughter, Dorothy, and her husband Robert Thrasher, also lived in Blanton's home for a while, and other family members lived next door. May lived until 1942 but never enjoyed good health after 1934, and Blanton helped care for her during those eight years, despite her own busy schedule.[54]

Blanton's closest sibling relationship in these years was with May, but she also stayed in contact with her other sister and brothers. She occasionally went to Dallas to visit her sister Faerie, who had married James Kilgore, a member of the faculty in the religion department at Southern Methodist University. From 1928, when Faerie suffered a series of strokes, until her death in 1930, Blanton spent as much time with her as her teaching duties allowed. Blanton communicated with her brothers less during these years, although she apparently was close to them. Her well-known brother Thomas, the only sibling to survive her, remained in Congress until 1936. Interestingly, his campaign for the U.S. Senate in 1928 placed him in a field that included, among others, former suffrage leader Minnie Fisher Cunningham. Cunningham had followed up her suffrage efforts with work in the League of Women Voters and the Democratic Party before entering the 1928 race and becoming the first Texas woman to make a bid for the U.S. Senate. If Annie Webb Blanton found it difficult to decide whether to support her brother or her old suffrage friend, she kept this to herself and openly showed no special interest in the race because firsthand political involvement was no longer her chief priority.[55]

However, interests that Blanton did maintain from her earlier years included her participation in numerous civic and educational groups, even while she was establishing and proving herself at the university. In addition to Delta Kappa Gamma, which became her highest priority outside the classroom after 1929, she was also active in the National Council of Administrative Women in Education, the American Association of University Professors, the American Association of University Women, and the National Sociological Society. She maintained her patriotic memberships in the Daughters of the American Revolution, for which she served as president of the Andrew Carruthers chapter in 1938, the United Daughters of the Confederacy, and the Daughters of the Republic of Texas. She served on the executive board of the Texas Federation of Women's Clubs, chairing the federation's committees on the Elimination of Illiteracy, Applied Education, and Department of Education. She spoke regularly at the federation's annual state conventions and in 1932 invited University of Texas President Benedict to speak before the group in Corpus Christi on "Problems of Higher Education." Her membership in Pi Lambda Theta, a scholastic organization for women educators, resulted in a statistical study of salaries of Texas college teachers. She was involved with other groups, though in a less active capacity, including the Texas Woman's Press Association, League of Women Voters, Texas Social Welfare Association, and First Methodist Church of Austin. Blanton's name appeared, along with some sixty others, on the letterhead of the Texas Commission on Inter-Racial Co-Operation in the 1920s, but there is no evidence that she took an active role in this group or shared ideals of racial change held by one of its leaders, her fellow Texan and suffragist Jessie Daniel Ames. Rather, Blanton's involvement appears to have been steeped in her general agreement with the group's desire to make social improvements in the South by recognizing the existence of a black middle class that could help resolve the region's ongoing racial disturbances — yet without challenging segregation or advocating racial equality.[56]

Beyond her organizational activities and family commitments, Blanton had other projects not directly associated with the university. In the 1930s she undertook research on the history of teacher certification in Texas, the progress of education in the state, and women school principals in the United States, although these works apparently were not published. Throughout her employment at Texas, she also spent part of most summers as a visiting professor at Our Lady of the Lake College in San Antonio, often returning to Austin in time to teach in the university's second summer session. She also occasionally participated in county institutes, where she taught individuals seeking their teacher certificates. Such work kept her busy, allowed her to teach, and provided a supplemental income. For many years she also spent some time answering regular inquiries she received from individuals across the state about a variety of educational concerns, happy to fill the role of experienced elder in matters pertaining to Texas schools.[57]

Blanton's post-superintendent years were full and productive. She established herself as a scholar in the state's foremost university, made pioneering contributions to the study of rural education, maintained her fight to improve Texas public schools, and continued her involvement in a variety of organizations. These years reflected Blanton's long and happy relationship with the University of Texas, as well as a certain self-distancing from politics. She also enjoyed being near her older sister and never complained of the familial responsibilities that returned to her in those later years.

The matured and experienced Blanton that emerged during this time appears somewhat more mellow than the younger woman who had fought with her boss at North Texas, actively joined the fight for woman suffrage, taken on the incumbent state superintendent in 1918, and sought a seat in Congress four years later. Perhaps she was — or perhaps her chosen projects after 1922 were less dramatic and volatile — but she remained just as determined and committed to what she believed to be important. Though her specific goals may have changed during these years, her willingness to work extremely hard for what she believed in and to fight for Texas schools remained constant. Blanton continued to exemplify what opportunities could be pursued — even if they were not all to be successful — by a woman who consistently placed herself in the public sphere. She never ceased in her efforts, despite the barriers she encountered, and she capitalized on the opportunities that came her way. Certainly society afforded her choices that women preceding her had not had, but not every woman was willing to fight as hard to take advantage of such opportunities. As one young southern woman noted in 1925, even with the positive changes that had unfolded for women in recent years, it took a woman of extraordinary ability and energy to establish a life that focused on professional accomplishment.[58]

Consistent with her feminist persuasions, Blanton's concerns for such accomplishment extended to other women teachers. After leaving public office she was reminded firsthand of the limits that remained for women professionals, and she continued to consider this problem as much more than a personal, individual one. Blanton knew that throughout her life she had benefited from the support of women's organizations and the personal relationships that evolved from them. The potential of such a group to help confront gender discrimination gradually convinced her of the need for a new, professional society for women educators. In 1929, this conviction led her to undertake what would be the most important organizational effort of her life. The founding of Delta Kappa Gamma and Blanton's involvement with it complete the picture of her unique contributions to education and to women and merit separate consideration.

Delta Kappa Gamma

1 9 2 9 - 4 5

"The Founders were strongly of the opinion that an organized body of women teachers selected from among the best in the profession united by bonds of friendship and by the force of common purposes—for the betterment of women teachers and the improvement of schools generally—would have an opportunity for rendering real service to education."[1] So wrote the founder of Delta Kappa Gamma in 1936, when the organization was seven years old. As always, she carefully credited all of the founders with what was, in fact, initially her own goal. Throughout her relationship with Delta Kappa Gamma, Annie Webb Blanton often initiated the plans that then became the larger objectives of the group. She struck a cautious balance: always first among equals, she used her undisputed leadership role to prove herself a successful and persuasive organizer.

Fewer than six years after joining the University of Texas faculty, and in the midst of her struggle to maintain a rural education department at the university, Annie Webb Blanton founded Delta Kappa Gamma. From 1929 until her death in 1945, Blanton dominated this honorary society for women educators, and through it her national prominence and exposure among women teachers increased well beyond the bounds of politics and academia.[2] Blanton created Delta Kappa Gamma in response to a variety of experiences and ideas she had, not as the result of a specific event, and she based the organization on a unique combination of feminism, femininity, and meritocracy. It encompassed various interests for her: her belief in clubs and associations as a means to effect change, her devotion to the teaching profession and the place of women in it, and her specific commitment to improve opportunities for female educators. The organization gave expression to Blanton's feminine, even maternal, nature.

The creation of Delta Kappa Gamma reflected Blanton's involvement, since her earlier years at North Texas, in women's clubs. Blanton had been instrumental in founding the City Federation of Women's Clubs in Denton and also had been a leader in that town's Woman's Shakespeare Club. Later, in Denton and Austin, she assumed an active role in a variety of other organizations for women, including those with civic and academic emphases.[3]

Such organizations usually focused on educational and self-improvement goals, rather than mere social interaction. Their development in Texas can be traced to earlier nineteenth-century literary clubs in the Northeast that proliferated from the 1870s, including such prominent women's clubs as Sorosis in New York City and the New England Woman's Club in Boston. By the 1880s, clubs for women had become common in the South, and, within another ten years, more political and civic concerns had supplanted their initial literary and educational emphases. The Texas Federation of Women's Clubs, an umbrella organization for numerous groups in the state, was created in 1897, patterning itself after the national General Federation of Women's Clubs, which had been formed several years earlier. By 1905, more than five thousand women in Texas were involved in some two hundred clubs in the state. Most of these organizations were progressive in certain respects: they advocated a role for women in the public sphere, supported such causes as woman suffrage and greater educational opportunities for females, and provided women with experience in leadership roles. At the same time, they embraced a traditional ideology of women as moral guardians, recognized the home as an influential contributor to morality, and projected a certain sense of elitism, joining middle- and upper-class white women who wished to pursue personal or societal improvement. By the time Blanton had become involved in club work, these organizations espoused two themes: commitment to extend women's influence and to improve society through utilization of women's abilities.[4]

These themes were consistent with Blanton's own beliefs, and she found club work rewarding. Moreover, because clubs often emphasized educational reform, Blanton found it especially natural and comfortable to participate in them, often in leadership roles. Her friendship with Anna Pennybacker, who served as president of both the state and national federations of women's clubs, the interaction and support that Blanton shared with Texas club women when she ran for office in 1918, and her continued involvement with the Texas Federation and other clubs after joining the University of Texas faculty, all indicate the consistent influence of such groups in her life.[5] Blanton actively participated in and benefited from the organized efforts of these clubs, and she understood, as historian Anne Firor Scott later wrote, that "the power of association had its own inner dynamic."[6] These clubs offered a network of communication about issues important to women; they emphasized organizational and leadership skills; and they were socially acceptable. In 1929, when she founded Delta Kappa Gamma, Blanton sought similarly broad results but within a more specific framework.[7]

The 1920s afforded an important social and political role for women's clubs. Building upon the organizational efforts they had made in their work for voting rights, groups such as the Texas Federation, the Women's Christian Temperance Union, the Congress of Mothers, and the League of Women Voters continued their civic role. In Texas, the Women's Joint Legislative Council, nicknamed the Petticoat Lobby, grew from a coalition of women's organizations, and focused on and achieved legislative reform in infant and maternal health care, emergency school appropriations, and prison and prohibition laws. Nationally, the Women's Joint Congressional Committee, led by Maud Wood Park, coordinated ten women's groups and served as a lobbying organization in Washington. Working with Julia Lathrop and the Children's Bureau, the committee achieved passage of the first social welfare legislation in the country's history, the Sheppard-Towner Maternity and Infancy Act of 1921. Thus during the 1920s in Texas, as throughout the country, women's clubs continued to pursue an agenda of Progressive reform within the social mainstream. In keeping with their maintenance of social acceptability, these clubs almost always were racially segregated, meaning that nonwhite women interested in club work had to form their own similar, but separate, organizations. The Texas Association of Colored Women was organized in 1905, and in 1911 La Liga Femenil Mexicanista was created in Laredo. Similar national groups, such as the National Association of Colored Women and the black counterpart to the American Association of University Women, also existed.[8]

Blanton continued to advocate Progressive reform in the 1920s, but by this time she had turned away from politics, and her own involvement in the Petticoat Lobby appears to have been limited. Still, she continued to recognize the value of organizations and associations. Throughout the 1920s, while teaching at the university, she quietly formulated plans which she had thought about for some time to create a white women's organization that would be based upon her involvement in club work but that contained a professional, rather than a political, patriotic, or literary emphasis.[9]

Getting working women to affiliate on behalf of their gender was not without problems. Many professional women viewed connections to any group that emphasized their womanhood as detrimental to career advancement, especially if it advocated more equality for women and thus could be perceived by males as troublesome. Delta Kappa Gamma's quick growth appears to suggest that Blanton overcame this problem as she made her appeal to potential members, but, as will be shown, there was some concern initially that the organization would meet with scorn from male, and perhaps female, colleagues. Blanton was always carefully aware of potential criticism and negative reaction to her organization, but she also held firm in her belief in the potential effectiveness of women working together, underscoring her commitment to women in both emotional and practical terms.[10]

Although most women's clubs in the 1920s were not designed to address the specific needs of professional women, a few notable exceptions existed. The National Federation of Business and Professional Women's Clubs had been founded in 1919 to join "women who individually had exercised so great an influence yet who were as a class non-gregarious."[11] Teachers joined this federation, although clerical workers were its mainstay. Teachers and other career women who lived in urban areas often joined women's city clubs, which provided opportunities for educational work, municipal reform efforts, and socializing. In addition, the American Association of University Women provided organizational sisterhood for women educators from the elementary to the college level.[12]

By founding Delta Kappa Gamma, Blanton did not seek to duplicate or to replace the efforts of these or any other groups, but rather to build on her own club and associational experiences by creating a distinctive society for women teachers which would, quite simply, remove barriers that limited their professional opportunities. Some who knew her believed that Blanton never forgot her younger brother telling her as a child that she could not become a lawyer because she was a girl, and others have speculated that Blanton longed to be a sorority member, an opportunity not available when she attended the University of Texas. Certainly these experiences may have contributed to her organization of Delta Kappa Gamma, but there was more to her motivations. From her Denton days, when her life-style had encompassed close professional and personal interaction with competent female colleagues, Blanton had found the company of such women enjoyable and stimulating and had recognized that women educators with similar interests and capabilities constituted a potentially powerful group if they could be organized. After Delta Kappa Gamma's creation, Blanton recalled that during her tenure as state superintendent a male colleague had told her that women's inability to stand together was hurting the teaching profession and the quality of education in Texas. This encounter reinforced her initial thoughts about the need for a group such as Delta Kappa Gamma, although it took several more years for her idea for an organization to mature.[13] She traced the evolution this way:

I saw that women in their progress towards equality with men, educationally and politically, had won each step in advancement by the demands of groups of intrepid women who did stand together. I thought that if we are to learn leadership, it must be chiefly in women's organizations. Finally I evolved the idea that we might accomplish more through a special organization working together for what women teachers especially need. This, I thought, should be composed of experienced teachers, more or less permanently in the profession. It seemed to me that such an organization would be more likely to succeed, if the ties binding its members together were rather close, and thus evolved the idea of a professional fraternity for women teachers.[14]

A key to understanding Delta Kappa Gamma and Blanton's involvement in it lies in recognizing her consistency in showing little direct interest in women who planned to teach only briefly, women who were unwilling to work hard, or women who were not of her own class and race. Her sense of gratitude to those successful, professional women who had gone before her was also important. She realized that even though society in the twentieth century accepted and approved women's role as educators, there was still some distance to go before women could attain true professional status and equality. Her desire to utilize her insights and experiences in order to help a larger, if still narrowly defined, group of women demonstrated the feminist drive within her to reduce the domination of males in the teaching profession by preparing women to improve, advance, and lead as teachers.[15]

Blanton believed her plans would be successful only if she sought members who were committed to teaching as a profession and who were willing to exert the time and energy necessary for the cause of her society. A sense of feminist meritocracy, then, inspired her ambitions. She also believed that by including in the new organization representatives from all levels of the teaching profession, she would be better able to foster understanding and mutual appreciation among women teachers. From her earliest dreams about the society, Blanton had envisioned a distinguished group of female educators whose joint efforts would result in both increased opportunities and long overdue recognition for women teachers, who since before the turn of the century, had comprised the majority of the teaching profession. Blanton's desire to help highly motivated, competent women reflected her feminist persuasions as well as her lifelong preference for the company of such individuals and her indifference to women she considered slackers. Her vision for the organization included a social dimension, but as with the other women's clubs with which she was associated, that was not the primary goal.[16]

Before seeking potential members for the new organization, Blanton carefully thought through some other specific goals she wished to pursue. Within the broad framework of advancing women educators and emphasizing unity, Blanton particularly wanted to improve academic opportunities for women and therefore she wanted the society to maintain a scholarship fund to allow members to continue their education. In the name of professionalism and to avoid duplicating or competing with such scholarly societies as Phi Beta Kappa or Pi Lambda Theta, she chose to emphasize experience over scholarship as a membership criteria. It was more important to Blanton to provide an opportunity for deserving women to improve themselves academically than to honor those with a certain scholastic record. She knew, from personal experience, the difficulties involved in pursuing degrees while holding full-time jobs, and she was genuinely concerned to make this process easier for other women.[17]

These desires and dreams, as they took shape in Blanton's mind during the late 1920s, continued to reinforce three basic beliefs she had long held: that merit, not gender, should determine leadership roles in education, that cooperative efforts were almost always positive, and that the potential of feminine leadership was unlimited. By 1929 she was certain that the new organization she envisioned could succeed in creating a professional spirit among women educators, recognizing outstanding teachers, providing scholarship opportunities, and lending direct support to legislation helpful to the interests of education and of women teachers.

Just as she faced challenges in other areas of her life with a determined commitment and an unwavering sense of the correctness of her goals, Blanton planned and executed her newest undertaking with energy and confidence, though she remained realistically aware of the magnitude of her ambition. The potential of an organization that allowed her to share her personal perspectives with professional colleagues excited her, and once it had been established, Delta Kappa Gamma remained an endeavor that uniquely merged Blanton's personal and professional lives. [18]

"We want all the feminine leaders of great reputation to embrace eagerly the opportunity of membership in our order; we want women to achieve in their work equal recognition with men, within a few years," Blanton wrote on the tenth anniversary of the group's founding. She realized that change might take longer than that but encouraged members with the thought that "within another decade, perhaps, we shall have made a beginning in lessening discriminations against women teachers" and in loosening the "stronghold of masculine privilege in work." [19] What she proposed, then, was rather uncommon for its time, and it encompassed Blanton's belief that deserving women could emphasize their femininity—their differences from men—without having to accept professional inequality or lesser career aspirations. What she sought, a close friend later observed, was simply a "place for women in the sun." [20] This approach of seeking greater opportunities for competent women within a context of traditional femininity paralleled her previous endeavors and feminist concerns.

Blanton's first step toward the actual founding of Delta Kappa Gamma was to approach potential members whose successful careers and professional attitudes indicated an appropriate character for her conceived organization. She wanted a small group, carefully chosen by herself, to join her as founders and to help her organize and enlarge the membership. Blanton used the contacts she had made during her career as a Texas educator to ensure that her cofounders represented a variety of educational positions and geographic regions within the state and were also women whom she knew and could judge personally. She listed fourteen women with whom she had worked during her career and sent each of them a letter outlining her plans. Even though all of the women she wrote lived in Texas, Blanton envisioned the organization becoming nationwide and presented her plans within this vein. Eleven women accepted Blanton's proposal and assisted her in preparing the group's constitution. Although it was difficult for these founders—and later, other members—to match consistently Blanton's commitment to Delta Kappa Gamma, the original members who joined her in 1929 played the significant role of confirming her ideas and energizing her plans. As she said, "There were none among the Founders who ridiculed my notion that we were about to begin a great organization for women teachers," adding that their faith strengthened her own courage and determination.[21]

Blanton's leadership role in the state teachers' association, her service as state superintendent, and her career at the university all served to set her apart from most women, and even most women educators, of her time. Nevertheless, she always sought personal and professional relationships with women whom she felt shared her own outlook, ideas, and, at least to some extent, professional experiences. As she moved forward with her plans for Delta Kappa Gamma, Blanton again turned to women very similar to herself, choosing as founders women with advanced degrees, leadership experience, and a clear sense of their roles as professionals. In relations with her eleven cofounders Blanton always remained the undisputed leader, but she was not otherwise very different from this small community. Her University of Texas colleagues who became Delta Kappa Gamma founders included Anna Hiss, associate professor of physical education and director of physical training for women; Helen Koch, psychology instructor; Ruby Terrill, dean of women and associate professor of classical languages; and Cora Martin, elementary education faculty member. Blanton was especially close to Martin and Terrill, with whom she was then sharing living quarters at the University Faculty Women's Club. Before the initiation ceremony for the founders, Martin joined Blanton in a careful study of Pi Lambda Theta, the scholarly education society for women to which they both belonged, to gather ideas for their new organization. Secondary history instructors (and sisters) Ray and Sue King of Fort Worth, and math teacher Lalla M. Odom of Austin joined these university women as founders. Elementary educators who accepted Blanton's invitation were Mamie Bastian, a principal in Houston; Ruby Cole, a San Antonio principal; Mabel Grizzard, a rural supervisor and teacher in Waxahachie; and Lela Lee Williams, an administrator for Dallas elementary schools.[22]

On Saturday, May 11, 1929, the new group met in the drawing

room of the University Faculty Women's Club in Austin, where Blanton initiated the women into Delta Kappa Gamma. The group elected Blanton as its first president, finalized its constitution, and organized committees to begin the work of incorporation and expansion.[23] Although the organization considered itself to be national in scope, the twelve members decided it best to limit their membership jurisdiction to Texas for several years before attempting broader growth. For its first four years, then, the founders and new members developed policies and procedures for local and statewide chapters. As national president from 1929 to 1933, Blanton assumed duties that included directing the efforts to organize new chapters in a plan for expansion that reflected her own original vision.[24]

To begin implementing this plan, select teachers from across the state were notified of Delta Kappa Gamma's founding. Then, in August, 1929, Blanton sent letters explaining the aims of the group to those who had expressed an interest. The correspondence explained that the new society would consist of women who had proven their success as teachers, shown leadership in professional organizations, and exhibited an unselfish professional spirit. To keep the society honorary, only up to a maximum of one-tenth of the total number of teachers in any school system or higher education facility would be admitted. Adding a bit of intrigue to the whole episode, Blanton selected a pseudonym with the initials "DKG" and signed the letters "Dalton Katherine Graham," in an effort, she later said, to keep male educators from learning of her plans and criticizing them. Her secrecy indicates that Blanton had anticipated male criticism, but no evidence remains as to which specific individuals she expected to be troublesome. Reminiscent of her fears of the teachers' machine while she had served as state superintendent, Blanton appears to have perceived some broad threat rather than any particular challenge. There probably were men who were eager to criticize an organization such as Delta Kappa Gamma, just as they had criticized a female state superintendent of public instruction; but to assume that the criticisms were serious enough to threaten careers, as Blanton implied, is not supported by historical evidence, particularly in her own case.[25]

In fact, Blanton's situation at the University of Texas was a positive factor in enabling her to establish Delta Kappa Gamma. By 1929, she had developed a comfortable relationship with the university and was in no jeopardy of losing her position, even though her rural education department was being phased out. Blanton apparently waited to proceed with her plans for Delta Kappa Gamma until she had completed her advanced degrees and attained professional security. The university provided her with these opportunities, and when she was ready to form her organization, she had the added benefit of choosing cofounders from among her immediate colleagues. The atmosphere of the Faculty Women's Club, into which Blanton had moved several years after joining the university faculty, was conducive to planning and holding ceremonies and meetings. It served as Delta Kappa Gamma headquarters until August, 1934, when Blanton purchased her own home in Austin and moved the organization there. Throughout the time of her involvement with the group, Blanton had the full support of her immediate male colleagues — those within the education department, as well as higher university officials. She never experienced difficulty in obtaining approval for absences related to Delta Kappa Gamma travel or other commitments.[26]

As Delta Kappa Gamma and her teaching duties both consumed a great deal of her time, it was to Blanton's advantage that she could concentrate on both without the two efforts conflicting. The university consistently supported her, as evidenced by a 1940 letter from Dean Pittenger of the school of education to university President Rainey, recommending approval of Blanton's request for a rather long absence in order to organize Delta Kappa Gamma chapters in the Northwest. "I am suggesting its approval for two reasons: first, I believe that the development of this organization which now enlists several thousand of the leading women educators in almost every state; and which was originated and promoted by Professor Blanton personally, is a real contribution to American education," Pittenger wrote. "Secondly," he added, "I feel that Miss Blanton's long and effective service to the state of Texas warrants this consideration."[27]

In the early years of Delta Kappa Gamma, Blanton busied

herself with every aspect of the new society, from soliciting members and organizing chapters to designing the membership key and making the first initiation scarf. She assisted Cora Martin in writing a song for the society and also organized the financial structure for the organization. Blanton gradually began to share many of these duties with the cofounders, and she relied heavily on their input. But when it came to actually proposing a plan of action and carrying it out, Blanton proved a singular force of leadership, especially during Delta Kappa Gamma's first few years. The death of Sue King and Helen Koch's move to Chicago soon after Delta Kappa Gamma's creation left only nine founders to assist Blanton as the group began its second year. At that time Blanton determined that she was best suited to concentrate on the group's expansion efforts throughout Texas and then into other states, while the other founders could deal primarily with internal efforts, such as formulating annual programs of work to facilitate better female representation in the state teachers' association and studying the feasibility of a retirement fund for teachers — issues bearing a strong resemblance to earlier Blanton causes. Even though Blanton occasionally complained that the nine founders were not giving enough of themselves to Delta Kappa Gamma, the distribution of work presented no major problems for the organization and probably could have existed no other way given Blanton's strong personality and conviction about the work of the group.[28]

By 1933 Blanton's effort to expand the organization had resulted in forty-seven Delta Kappa Gamma chapters in Texas, Alabama, Oklahoma, and Missouri, with a total membership of fifteen hundred women. State conventions were held annually, and continued growth seemed assured. Blanton noted that some men believed the organization existed to fight them and many women not asked to join resented Delta Kappa Gamma, but "we all learned to laugh at checks and criticism, and go calmly ahead." By this time Blanton knew that Delta Kappa Gamma would fulfill the dreams she had for the organization and that the risks and chances of failure had been successfully minimized. She believed that the success stemmed from her own contacts, hard work, and attention to detail — her letters of instruction to new chapters often ran to twenty-five pages in longhand—as well as the continued addition of the right kind of members, often with the advice of local male school superintendents and university officials. And, the success of the first few years had motivated her to aim for even greater growth in the future.[29]

In 1933 Blanton decided that her term as national president would end after four years, rather than the originally scheduled six. The change, however, did not reflect any decrease in her commitment to Delta Kappa Gamma, but rather indicated her desire to have a non-Texan become president in order to aid in expansion efforts and to allow herself to take on new duties for the growing group. From 1933 to 1945 Blanton held no official office, but her control of Delta Kappa Gamma remained intact: she served as executive secretary—first on the state level, then on the national—and thus kept the group's headquarters in her home from 1934 until several months before her death in 1945; she was editor of the organization's *Bulletin,* which had begun officially in 1934; and she was directly involved in the selection of state and national officers.[30]

Blanton's emotional and physical involvement in Delta Kappa Gamma in these years was deeply intense, but she did obtain her desired results. She inaugurated the group's scholarship fund, created an annual achievement award, and projected the group's expansion into foreign countries. Membership included the most prominent female educators, including those who served as state superintendents across the country and numerous women who were leaders in the National Education Association. Blanton continued to travel and to organize new chapters, and at her death Delta Kappa Gamma existed in all forty-eight states and Washington, D.C., with a total membership of almost twenty-three thousand; thirty-five states had been organized by Blanton alone. This growth brought increased financial security to the group, and in 1940 a lot was purchased near downtown Austin to be the future site for a new headquarters building. She also saw the group continue its work on behalf of teachers' retirement funds and salary equity for women teachers. The eventual success with these issues cannot be attributed solely to Delta Kappa Gamma; nevertheless, the organization was a very important contributor, especially as it grew and increased in numbers and strong visible leaders.

As the organization flourished, its members acknowledged Blanton's personal commitment in many ways. They endowed a scholarship in her name, gave her the group's first national achievement award, had her portrait painted for the planned new headquarters, gave her monetary gifts in appreciation of her personal time and financial sacrifice to the group, presented her with a scrapbook of letters and other organizational memorabilia, and purchased a car in order to assist her in her travels to organize new chapters and states. All of these expressions of appreciation were extremely meaningful to Blanton. It suited her to work hard for her organization, but she needed to know, especially from this group to which she increasingly devoted almost all her extra time, that her efforts were appreciated. These personal signs of gratitude showed that she was not taken for granted. Blanton maintained that she and the other founders were average, not great, women, who needed no special appreciation for their work with Delta Kappa Gamma. However, based on her response to the organization's expressions of gratitude, it would appear that appreciation for her efforts was more important than she herself admitted.[31]

Blanton never hesitated to indicate her gratitude for such recognition, as in this 1939 response in the *Bulletin* to the presentation of her new car: "I thought when, in Chicago, you gave me the priceless book of letters, there was nothing more that anyone could do for me. But I did not fully understand the resourcefulness of Delta Kappa Gamma members — their vivid imagination and generous hearts. I can think of nothing material that will give me more pleasure than a new car. Its name is Prudence (I always name my cars) and it is a Chevrolet sedan, 1940 model, beige color. [I] appreciate and love you all, and [will] remember, as long as I live, how you celebrated our tenth anniversary."[32] Blanton, who had learned to drive only later in her life, thoroughly enjoyed this automobile. Her family often worried about her driving, and one former student has recalled the horrors of being in a car driven by Blanton in the hills west of Austin. However, she apparently avoided any serious mishaps on her frequent travels.[33]

PRUDENCE AND I SEND GREETINGS
A MERRY CHRISTMAS AND
A HAPPY NEW YEAR
Annie Webb Blanton

Blanton and her beloved car "Prudence." This photo was taken soon after Delta Kappa Gamma presented this car to Blanton in 1939, in appreciation of her work for the organization. (Photo courtesy Special Collections Library, Texas Woman's University.)

In addition to providing Blanton with an opportunity to use her leadership skills and pursue her goals for women teachers, as well as giving her a sense of personal and professional reward for her efforts, Delta Kappa Gamma also became a significant outlet for Blanton to express her feminine and maternal traits within the realm of professionalism. Blanton expressed no regret at having never married, but she clearly loved children and doted on her younger siblings, nieces and nephews, and other youngsters in her family. She was also a woman to whom a lovely home, domestic skills, and other traditionally feminine touches were very important. She once noted that she enjoyed wearing earrings because "they always seem to me to express the frivolous side of my nature—a side quite disappointing to some of my dignified friends." Within Delta Kappa Gamma, Blanton showed these emotions and preferences in ways not clearly evi-

dent in her classroom or other career endeavors. She emphasized to the group the importance of wearing its selected jewelry
and of dressing properly at all times. To honor pioneer women
educators she began a collection of dolls dressed in period cos-
tumes, which she displayed at each annual convention. As editor of the *Bulletin,* she included articles on the value of literature,
music, and social activities for members and also ran baby pictures of the original founders.[34]

Blanton's writings in the *Bulletin* frequently referred to her
maternal relationship to the group and included the range of roles
inherent in parental relationships. She scolded members for sub-
mitting information incorrectly to the *Bulletin* and fussed when
they demonstrated irresponsibility regarding their membership
duties. She complained when members were late with initiation
reservations and *Bulletin* information.[35] Tired of receiving endless queries herself for information about the organization that
was available elsewhere, she wrote to chapter and state presidents
in 1939: "If I had the time, I would gladly give every one of our
members all the help and information that she needs so far as
I have ability. But I am, like yourselves, a very busy teacher. I
teach six days a week. I give tests and grade them. I do correspondence teaching. I work in faculty committees. I direct graduate theses—I earn my living, just as you do. I can edit the *Bulletin,*
keep accounts of indebtedness for 33 states and 250 chapters, and
supervise the sending out of materials. I can work on the organization of new states. But this is *all* that I can do."[36]

Conversely, she could take the role of proud and boastful par-
ent, referring to new chapters as young offspring in need of care,
calling herself and enjoying being called Delta Kappa Gamma's
"mother."[37] In 1939, she wrote of Delta Kappa Gamma, "A mother
who has several children who express their affection and appreciate her past efforts is fortunate; but what of the mother who
has 10,000 'children,' who delight to do her honor!"[38] And five
years later, shortly before her death, she observed, "Like all dot-
ing mothers, I have often looked upon you, as too wonderful to
be true."[39] She could also encourage members and take pride in
them, and herself, because of their accomplishments, as she did
in a 1939 editorial of the *Bulletin:* "Delta Kappa Gamma must

have filled a felt need or it could not have grown so rapidly. And its prestige must be established in each new state, by the character of our members, by the purposes for which we exist, by the worthwhile activities in which we engage, by the beauty of the fellowship which animates our personal relationships."[40]

This aspect of Blanton's interaction with Delta Kappa Gamma suggests that in many ways the society had become her extended family. Her closest friends were members, and almost all her social activities related to Delta Kappa Gamma. It was not that the organization replaced any other part of her life; after Delta Kappa Gamma was founded, she still actively maintained her teaching duties and university involvement, her scholarly endeavors, her interest in rural education, her familial responsibilities, and her memberships in other organizations. Rather, it was that the society fulfilled a need in a part of her life that was not quite complete and comfortably allowed her to be her most feminine self. It provided a widening enhancement of the friendships with women that had long been important to her; it created opportunities for family-like relationships; and it gave her a sense that her efforts and ideas might continue after her death.[41]

The members of Delta Kappa Gamma took Blanton's dominance in stride, dwelling on her positive contributions and usually understanding when she encouraged them to do better. When the first volume of the organization's official history appeared in 1960, grateful appreciation to Blanton was expressed, and this explanation of her approach to the group was included: "If at times she was possessive, it was normal for her to be protective of her progeny; if positive in her opinions, it was because her experiences had been so broad; if exacting, it was because she expected above average response from the upper ten percent of the profession; if ambitious, it was because of her great hopes for the usefulness of The Delta Kappa Gamma Society."[42]

Blanton's relationship with Delta Kappa Gamma was a constant and increasingly important factor in her life after 1929. Still, she maintained her regular teaching duties until 1940, when the state required her to retire to modified service. Delta Kappa Gamma helped Blanton cope with her undesired retirement by offering to pay her a half-time salary for the work she was already doing as the group's executive secretary. The money helped, but the gesture was more important for its reaffirmation that Blanton's services were still needed and worthy of payment. Blanton's full-time teaching load had not been problematic for her throughout the 1930s, as she carried out her Delta Kappa Gamma duties, but the new half-time teaching arrangement did have the advantage of making it easier for Blanton to travel long-distance, which had become increasingly necessary as the society expanded across the country. Subsequently, her requests to the university for travel time for the society increased after 1940, as she organized chapters and attended meetings throughout Texas and in numerous other states, including Wyoming, Montana, Idaho, Oregon, Nevada, Minnesota, Delaware, and Arkansas. Blanton conscientiously maintained her classroom duties during that time, but she clearly thrived on the Delta Kappa Gamma trips and exhibited her usual abundance of energy to remain active in the years after her seventieth birthday.[43]

Blanton's energy and the group's solid foundation allowed Delta Kappa Gamma to continue its growth in the 1940s, even through World War II. Blanton occasionally cancelled travel plans when civilian train travel became too uncertain during wartime and postponed construction of the group's headquarters until after the war. Delta Kappa Gamma responded to the world crisis with a war bonds project and encouraged its members to remain committed to the organization throughout the conflict, while making necessary patriotic sacrifices.[44]

The toll of years of activity and intense commitment to numerous causes, especially to Delta Kappa Gamma, only gradually began to slow Blanton in the 1940s. In 1941 she determined that after 1945 she would no longer serve as executive secretary for the organization and might also retire from her remaining teaching duties. Whether she could have lived a happy life in full retirement is debatable, but by declaring her intention to decrease her organizational duties after 1945, Blanton wisely allowed time for the society to plan for future leadership without immediately diminishing her own role. This planning, as well as the structure of national officers already in place, allowed for an easy transition upon Blanton's death in 1945. Blanton also re-

Annie Webb Blanton in academic regalia, including a Delta Kappa Gamma necklace, in 1941. (Photo courtesy The Delta Kappa Gamma Society International, copyright 1960.)

arranged her domestic situation in the early 1940s. Following the deaths of her sister and brother-in-law, May and Frank Hill, she sold the Austin home she had shared with them and moved to their former country home just outside Austin. This residence had been inherited by the Hills' daughter, Dorothy, who with her husband Robert Thrasher had renovated and enlarged the dwelling. They eagerly invited their aunt to live with them. Blanton was especially close to her niece, who was in many ways like a daughter to her, and found sharing a home with Dorothy in these latter years of her life to be an ideal arrangement. This move, along with periodic vacations in the Davis Mountains of West Texas, invigorated Blanton and eased some minor complaints from arthritis. She continued her travels for Delta Kappa Gamma and her classroom work without interruption until the spring of 1945, when, at age seventy-four, she began to suffer serious complications from intestinal influenza and heart problems. By May of that year, however, she was somewhat improved and made plans, ultimately unfulfilled, to attend Delta Kappa Gamma's national convention scheduled for August in Denver. She also held a luncheon in her home for members of Austin's Delta Kappa Gamma chapter and prepared her final edition of the *Bulletin*. Still committed to the integrity of the University of Texas, she also signed a petition prepared by faculty members stating that tenure and academic freedom remained secure at the university, despite the recent controversy concerning the board of regents' firing of President Rainey.[45]

Blanton's health gradually declined through the summer, however. On July 20, 1945, in handwriting barely legible, Blanton submitted a brief letter to Drs. Ayer and Pittenger of the school of education, which requested permission to resign upon doctor's orders. Even as she neared the end of her life, Blanton maintained her dignity, awareness, and professionalism, requesting that the university process her resignation by August 1 to enable her to draw immediately on her teachers' retirement fund.[46] The university complied, announcing her retirement in September, along with praise for her past services as state superintendent, Delta Kappa Gamma founder, and university leader in rural education.[47]

On October 2, 1945, a little more than a month after her seventy-fifth birthday, Blanton died from a cerebral hemorrhage and arteriosclerosis at her country home. She was buried in the family plot in Austin's Oakwood Cemetery, and at the burial each Delta Kappa Gamma member present placed a red rose on her casket.

Her estate, valued at about seven thousand dollars, was left to her niece Dorothy Thrasher.[48]

The significance of Blanton's contributions to education and women teachers did not need the passage of time to manifest itself. Largely because of her Delta Kappa Gamma work, she was well-known among educators throughout the country. Telegrams, letters, and resolutions from individuals and Delta Kappa Gamma chapters poured into Thrasher's home upon Blanton's death. They expressed a sense of Blanton's friendship and sisterhood, her ability to turn her concern for women into a tangible legacy, and the vision evident in such an endeavor. At her death, the accomplishments of Delta Kappa Gamma were clear. A strong committee system kept the organization involved in issues pertaining to equal opportunity and increased visibility for women teachers, as well as major education issues. Annual conventions provided opportunities to meet colleagues from around the country and to hear such prominent speakers as Mary Ritter Beard and Judge Sarah T. Hughes. A state and national scholarship program was in place to aid members in pursuit of graduate work.[49]

Upon her death, the *Delta Kappa Gamma Bulletin* noted that the organization was Blanton's greatest and most compelling interest, as well as the realization of her greatest dream. Perhaps as meaningful for Blanton as seeing her dream fulfilled was knowing that the society she looked upon as a dear child would continue after her death and that the reforms she had worked for throughout her lifetime as an educator would continue to be addressed. Despite the domination of her strong personality in Delta Kappa Gamma for sixteen years, and despite the certainty and force with which she had made decisions in the organization, the group managed to extend itself beyond her personality and to move forward in the years after her death. In 1946, the group officially ended its policy of accepting only white women for membership. The 1950s witnessed Delta Kappa Gamma's move to new headquarters in Austin. By the early 1990s the society had more than 160,000 members in the United States and twelve other countries. International and state scholarships, an educational foundation, and annual awards provide continued monetary support to women teachers. In short, the ideas of professionalism encouraged by its founder continue to be addressed today.[50]

Delta Kappa Gamma became Blanton's greatest legacy, but it achieved its significance because of what she herself had previously attained. Without her record of public service to women and education, as well as her years of teaching experience and professional preparation, Blanton would have had little to offer the organization. Conversely, those experiences as president of the teachers' association, state superintendent, and university professor, though worthwhile in their own right, would have limited her influence to a much smaller scale without the existence of Delta Kappa Gamma. The culmination of the organization and her lifetime of professionalism combined to produce a woman of unique influence. Delta Kappa Gamma succeeded not only because Blanton used her energy and influence to nurture it, but also because she recognized the need for emphasizing women's role as professional educators. Astutely incorporating both feminism and femininity into the organization, Blanton created a long-lasting society with unique historical significance. She built on women's traditionally accepted role in the classroom to move women educators several steps closer to professional equality.

Conclusion

Soon after Annie Webb Blanton died in 1945, her University of Texas colleagues passed a memorial resolution which noted, "The personality of one who is a breaker of so many precedents invites analysis."[1] It was this role as a precedent-breaker, an invader of male privilege, that established Blanton in the state's political and educational circles. Once there, she proved capable of using her talents to effect positive changes for Texas schools.

That part of Blanton's life, however, gives less than a complete picture of the woman. Her career can be fully understood only when one sees that, in every position she held and every recognition she received, she was determined to bring along her women colleagues, whom she believed had earned equal rights. Drawing strength and support from close female teacher friends, Blanton had as her most abiding concern the improvement of conditions for deserving white women educators. Better professional standards for women, she believed, would create better schools. Leadership came naturally to her, and she capitalized on her ability to encourage and motivate others. While she had great appreciation for the few role models who existed across the country as female leaders in education, as well as for those women educational reformers whose careers had preceded her own, Blanton's concerns focused on the direct influence and interaction she shared with her own colleagues and friends. She believed the future would hold great potential if capable women worked together, and she devoted her life to that end.

Blanton benefited from two important forces. First, and most personally, she was a woman of consistent convictions and loyalty. The efforts that she exerted in Delta Kappa Gamma follow directly from the reforms she had advocated as president of the state teachers' association in 1917. While she matured and learned from her experiences, Blanton never underwent a drastic change in her educational philosophy, her belief in women's ability to prove themselves, her devotion to the South and to the University of Texas, or her social convictions. Such consistency is not necessarily a virtue, but for Blanton it seemed to exist without dangerous obstinacy and allowed her to make tangible progress as an educational and feminist reformer.

The second—and more public—force that aided Blanton was the timing of her efforts. She established herself professionally as an educator in Denton at the height of the Progressive era, when advocacy of school reform and suffrage enjoyed some prominence. This aura of the early 1900s provided an opening for her that would be essential to her later success, while allowing her to be both progressive and traditional; it is in the tension between these two characteristics that she found a comfortable leadership role. It was a time when reformism and elitism co-existed, and few Progressive leaders then would have criticized the narrow social focus of Blanton's endeavors. She lived and worked, as did most all of her fellow reformers in Texas, within a white, middle-class world, with no desire to extend her personal or professional efforts beyond it.

Consistency and opportunity characterized Blanton's career. To these forces she brought her determination to assist proven women educators to achieve equality, professionalism, and the benefits of working together. In Texas, these efforts established her as the state's most significant female educator of this century. As the state today continues its search for a better school system and as women continue to seek a sense of professional equality, the contributions of Annie Webb Blanton remain fixed in Texas history, providing both a reminder of how social context defines reform and an example of a Progressive feminist spirit.

Notes

PREFACE

1. Some biographical material on Blanton generated by Delta Kappa Gamma is found in Eunah Temple Holden, *Our Heritage in the Delta Kappa Gamma Society,* 1:17–22, 2:3–20; and Clara M. Parker, *Annie Webb Blanton, Founder: The Delta Kappa Gamma Society.* Short articles on Blanton's professional career include "A Tribute to Dr. Annie Webb Blanton, National Founder of the Delta Kappa Gamma Society, Program Presented at Opening of Annie Webb Blanton Dormitory at the University of Texas, Sept. 25, 1955" (copy in Annie Webb Blanton Biographical File, Austin History Center); and Arnie Weissman, "Annie Webb Blanton," *Texas Outlook* 65 (Winter, 1981–82): 21. Blanton is also mentioned in Ruthe Winegarten and Judith N. McArthur, eds., *Citizens at Last: The Woman Suffrage Movement in Texas,* pp. 172, 174–75; Janet G. Humphrey, *A Texas Suffragist: Diaries and Writings of Jane Y. McCallum,* pp. 112, 119, 150; Ann Fears Crawford and Crystal Sasse Ragsdale, *Women in Texas: Their Lives, Their Experiences, Their Accomplishments,* pp. 191–201; and Ruthe Winegarten, *Texas Women: A Pictorial History from Indians to Astronauts,* pp. 65, 116, 143.

2. See for example *Dallas Morning News,* July 28, 1990, Feb. 27, 1991; *Austin American-Statesman,* July 21, 1990; Feb. 16, 1992. The State Purchasing and General Services Commission named the building for William P. Clements in February, 1991, according to the records of the Texas Historical Commission.

3. See for example *Dallas Morning News,* Feb. 21, 22, 1991.

INTRODUCTION

1. Quotes from Blanton are from *Texas School Journal* 37 (Oct., 1919): 9. This discussion of feminism draws on numerous significant works that consider how the term is defined and used by historians. See, for example, Nancy F. Cott, *The Grounding of Modern Feminism,* pp. 4–5;

Cott, "What's in a Name? The Limits of 'Social Feminism'; or, Expanding the Vocabulary of Women's History," *Journal of American History* 76 (Dec., 1989): 809–29; Sharon Sievers, "Dialogue: Six (or More) Feminists in Search of a Historian," *Journal of Women's History* 1 (Fall, 1989): 134–46; Karen Offen, "Defining Feminism: A Comparative Historical Approach," *Signs: Journal of Women in Culture and Society* 14 (Autumn, 1988): 119–57; Gerda Lerner, *The Majority Finds Its Past: Placing Women in History,* pp. 48–49; Karen J. Blair, *The Clubwoman as Feminist: True Womanhood Redefined, 1868–1914,* pp. 117–19.

CHAPTER 1

1. Standard Certificate of Death for Annie Webb Blanton; University of Texas President's File for Annie Webb Blanton.

2. Lawrence A. Cremin, *American Education: The National Experience, 1783–1876,* p. 511; Carl H. Moneyhon, "Public Education and Texas Reconstruction Politics, 1871–1874," *Southwestern Historical Quarterly* 92 (Jan., 1989): 393, 395; Frederick Eby, *The Development of Education in Texas,* p. 164.

3. Eby, *Development of Education,* pp. 149–51, 157, 173. The quote is from p. 157.

4. Henry Allen Bullock, *A History of Negro Education in the South from 1619 to the Present,* pp. 57–58; Moneyhon, "Public Education," p. 415; Eby, *Development of Education,* pp. 168, 173, 195; Thad Sitton and Milam C. Rowold, *Ringing the Children In: Texas Country Schools,* pp. 6–8; James D. Anderson, *The Education of Blacks in the South, 1860–1935,* pp. 4–5; Stewart D. Smith, "Schools and Schoolmen: Chapters in Texas Education, 1870–1900," Ph.D. diss., University of North Texas, 1974, pp. 4–5, 8–9, 12, 24–25, 27; Robert A. Calvert and Arnoldo De León, *The History of Texas,* pp. 149–50. The community school system in Texas was a voluntary arrangement where parents provided county judges with a list of pupils, the judge then named school trustees, and the trustees in turn hired teachers. These community schools evolved into rural common schools, while independent school districts developed in urban areas. (See Smith, "Schools and Schoolmen," pp. 24–25; Sitton and Rowold, *Ringing the Children In,* pp. 8–9.)

5. Patricia Albjerg Graham, "Expansion and Exclusion: A History of Women in American Higher Education," *Signs: Journal of Women in Culture and Society* 3 (Summer, 1978): 761, 762, 764; Susan Boslego Carter, "Academic Women Revisited: An Empirical Study of Changing Patterns in Women's Employment as College and University Faculty, 1890–1963," *Journal of Social History* 14 (Summer, 1981): 675; Helen Lefkowitz Horowitz, *Alma Mater: Design and Experience in the Women's Col-*

leges from Their Nineteenth Century Beginnings to the 1930s, pp. 9, 28, 42, 71, 95, 105, 134; Margaret Gribskov, "Adelaide Pollock and the Founding of the National Council of Administrative Women in Education," in Patricia A. Schmuck, ed., *Women Educators: Employees of Schools in Western Countries,* p. 125; Rosalind Rosenberg, "The Limits of Access: The History of Coeducation in America," in John Mack Faragher and Florence Howe, eds., *Women and Higher Education in American History,* pp. 109–10, 154.

6. Susan Ware, *Partner and I: Molly Dewson, Feminism, and New Deal Politics,* p. 33.

7. Patricia A. Palmieri, "Patterns of Achievement of Single Academic Women at Wellesley College, 1880–1920," *Frontiers: A Journal of Women Studies* 5 (Spring, 1980): 64; Ware, *Partner and I,* p. 16; Jacquelyn Dowd Hall, *Revolt against Chivalry: Jessie Daniel Ames and the Women's Campaign against Lynching,* pp. 8–9; Barbara Miller Solomon, *In the Company of Educated Women: A History of Women and Higher Education in America,* p. 61.

8. Annie's sister Fannie died as a teenager. Her sisters Faerie and May were homemakers. See Lennon J. Hill and K. Marie Watson Hill, *Isaac Hill, Sr. and His Descendants, 1748–1980,* pp. 44–47; Holden, *Our Heritage,* 1:17, 2:5. Information on her sisters was also provided through my interview with Margaret McDermott (a cousin of Blanton's) and James Kilgore (the son of Blanton's sister Faerie and her husband, James Kilgore), Dallas, Sept. 9, 1988.

9. Solomon, *In the Company,* p. 63.

10. Annie Webb Blanton to Minnie Fisher Cunningham, Mar. 20, 1918, MS74, 15/225, Minnie Fisher Cunningham Papers.

11. University of Texas President's File for Annie Webb Blanton; "Annie Webb Blanton Memorial Resolution," General Faculty Minutes, June 11, 1946, Annie Webb Blanton Vertical File, Barker Texas History Center, University of Texas, Austin; Hill and Hill, *Isaac Hill,* pp. 44–47; Holden, *Our Heritage,* 1:17, 2:11.

12. Holden, *Our Heritage,* 2:11–12; Asa Hill Historical Marker File, Texas Historical Commission, Austin; Hill and Hill, *Isaac Hill,* pp. 44–47; "Monument Hill State Historic Site," Brochure, Monument Hill State Historic Site; Walter P. Webb and H. B. Carroll, eds., *The Handbook of Texas,* 1:812–13, 2:392–93.

13. Asa Hill Historical Marker File; Hill and Hill, *Isaac Hill,* pp. 44–47; Delta Kappa Gamma Society, Alpha State Organization, *Pioneer Women Teachers of Texas,* pp. 5–7; "Brief Biography of Annie Webb Blanton," Annie Webb Blanton Vertical File; 2F40, Fayette County Ar-

chives, Barker Texas History Center; Holden, *Our Heritage,* 2:12; *Daily Houston Telegraph,* July 29, 1870–Apr. 6, 1875; *Members of the Legislature of the State of Texas from 1846 to 1939,* pp. 6–8; Eldon Stephen Branda, ed., *The Handbook of Texas,* 3:1091. Since Webb did not arrive in Texas until the end of the Republic era, references to his service as an officer in the war for Texas independence and as a member of the first Texas congress apparently are erroneous. (See Holden, *Our Heritage,* 1:17, 2:12; Parker, *Annie Webb Blanton, Founder,* p. 8; Hill and Hill, *Isaac Hill,* pp. 44–47.)

14. *Daily Houston Telegraph,* July 29, 1870.

15. Hill and Hill, *Isaac Hill,* pp. 44–47; Holden, *Our Heritage,* 2:12; Delta Kappa Gamma, *Pioneer Women Teachers of Texas,* pp. 5–7.

16. David G. McComb, *Houston: A History,* pp. 17, 19, 21, 35–36, 38, 40, 60; Holden, *Our Heritage,* 2:12; Hill and Hill, *Isaac Hill,* pp. 44–47.

17. Holden, *Our Heritage,* 2:10, 12; Annie Webb Blanton Historical Marker File, Texas Historical Commission; "Annie Webb Blanton Memorial," Records of Dallas Independent School District, p. 15; "Annie Webb Blanton Memorial Resolution," Annie Webb Blanton Vertical File; McComb, *Houston,* p. 41; McDermott and Kilgore interview; *Handbook of Texas,* 3:1091.

18. Hill and Hill, *Isaac Hill,* pp. 44–47; Delta Kappa Gamma, *Pioneer Women Teachers of Texas,* pp. 5–7; "Annie Webb Blanton Memorial," Dallas Independent School District, pp. 2–3; McDermott and Kilgore interview; author's interview with Eugenia Hill Ramsey (a great-niece of Blanton's), Austin, Oct. 23, 1988; Holden, *Our Heritage,* 1:17, 2:5. Blanton's paternal grandmother, who helped raise the children after their mother's death, must have had some influence on Annie in her young years, but little is known of this woman. Blanton made virtually no references to her, or to her own mother's death, that have survived in the historical record. Blanton's special relationship with May carried into the next generation. May's daughter, Dorothy Hill Thrasher, was much like a daughter to Annie Webb Blanton; Blanton lived her later years in Thrasher's home outside Austin and died there in 1945 (Ramsey interview; see also chapter 5 for a further discussion of this arrangement).

19. Hill and Hill, *Isaac Hill,* pp. 44–47; McDermott and Kilgore interview; Delta Kappa Gamma, *Pioneer Women Teachers of Texas,* pp. 5–7; Holden, *Our Heritage,* 2:5, 12; Blanton to O. H. Cooper, Mar. 6, 1929, Annie Webb Blanton Vertical File; *Daily Texan,* Apr. 2, 1954.

20. Delta Kappa Gamma, *Pioneer Women Teachers of Texas,* pp. 5–7; Blanton Historical Marker File; "Annie Webb Blanton Memorial,"

Dallas Independent School District, p. 12; "Annie Webb Blanton Memorial Resolution," Annie Webb Blanton Vertical File; Holden, *Our Heritage,* 2:12. Pine Springs is located off Farm Road 609, near Interstate 10 and the town of Flatonia. By the 1990s all that remained of the community was a small cemetery. The Pine Springs School closed in 1944, but in 1969, in commemoration of Blanton's first year of teaching there, a plaque was placed at the site of the school by Delta Kappa Gamma, the honorary society for women teachers that Blanton had founded in 1929. The plaque has since been removed by vandals. (Information from visit to Pine Springs, July 7, 1988, and correspondence from Liz Obelgoner, Fayette County Delta Kappa Gamma member, and Sylvia Seidenberger, the last teacher at Pine Springs School, July and August, 1988.)

21. Kathryn Kish Sklar, *Catharine Beecher: A Study in American Domesticity,* pp. 97–98, 173–74, 180–82, 222–23; Alice Kessler-Harris, *Out To Work: A History of Wage-Earning Women in the United States,* pp. 56, 68, 235; Leslie Woodcock Tentler, *Wage-Earning Women: Industrial Work and Family Life in the United States, 1900–1930,* pp. 1–2, 81–82. Tentler's work focuses on a social and economic class of women — those daughters in the working-class who often left school early in order to work in factories, stores, and offices — different from those who usually became teachers. While the majority of women who entered the work force in the country after 1875 fall into this category, the situation is not identical to the experiences of middle-class wage-earning women who became teachers.

22. Sarah Eisenstein, *Give Us Bread But Give Us Roses: Working Women's Consciousness in the United States, 1890 to the First World War,* p. 77. The first quote, cited by Eisenstein, is from Ella Rodman Church's 1882 book *Money-Making for Ladies.* The second quote is from Nancy Hoffman, *Women's "True" Profession: Voices from the History of Teaching,* p. xvii.

23. Parker, *Annie Webb Blanton, Founder,* p. 29 (quote); Annie Webb Blanton, *A Hand Book of Information as to Education in Texas, 1918–1922;* Blanton to Cooper, Mar. 6, 1929, Annie Webb Blanton Vertical File; B. F. Pittenger to W. M. W. Splawn, June 8, 1925, VF1/B, University of Texas President's Office Records; Instructional Load, School of Education, Fall Semester, 1927, VF1/B, University of Texas President's Office Records; Blanton to Pittenger, Feb. 2, 1928, VF1/A, University of Texas President's Office Records. Blanton's graduate studies at Cornell also focused on rural education, as is discussed in chapter 4.

24. Interview with Betty Murray (a student of Blanton's at the University of Texas in 1937), Harlingen, Aug. 15, 1987.

25. "Annie Webb Blanton, Democratic Candidate for Representative in Congress of the Thirteenth Congressional District," Handbill, 2M78, Mrs. Percy V. Pennybacker Papers.

26. McDermott and Kilgore interview; Ruth Lynn Williams, *Proudly She Serves,* p. 77; Delta Kappa Gamma, *Pioneer Women Teachers of Texas,* pp. 5–7; Blanton Historical Marker File; "Annie Webb Blanton Memorial Resolution," Annie Webb Blanton Vertical File; Parker, *Annie Webb Blanton, Founder,* pp. 9–10; *Handbook of Texas,* 3:1091. Holden, *Our Heritage,* 2:12, states that Blanton was too young to enter the University of Texas upon her graduation from high school and, therefore, had taken the job at Pine Springs. However, in 1884, the board of regents had approved a regulation that allowed both male and female students to be admitted as young as age sixteen; when she graduated from high school, Blanton had been almost seventeen. (See Roger A. Griffin, "To Establish a University of the First Class," *Southwestern Historical Quarterly* 86 [Oct., 1982]: 158.) Blanton's maternal grandmother, Sarah Ann Amelia Hill Webb, died in 1883 (Hill Historical Marker File).

27. "Annie Webb Blanton for State Superintendent of Public Instruction," Broadside, Annie Webb Blanton Vertical File; Employment Records of Annie Webb Blanton, Austin Independent School District; Blanton Historical Marker File; Holden, *Our Heritage,* 2:5; "Annie Webb Blanton, Democratic Candidate for Representative in Congress of the Thirteenth Congressional District," Handbill, 2M78, Pennybacker Papers. East Austin later was renamed Bickler Elementary and West Austin later became Pease Elementary.

28. *Handbook of Texas,* 2:821; Griffin, "To Establish a University of the First Class," pp. 135–60.

29. Employment Records of Annie Webb Blanton, Austin Independent School District; University of Texas President's File for Annie Webb Blanton. Several sources refer to Blanton as a special student at the university for five years before she was formally admitted, with junior status. (See Holden, *Our Heritage,* 2:17; Blanton Historical Marker File; "A Tribute to Dr. Annie Webb Blanton," Blanton Biographical File.) Margaret Berry, a former student of Blanton's at Texas and herself later an official of the university, told me that the special status resulted from LaGrange High School's lack of accreditation with the University of Texas as an approved secondary school (interview with Margaret Berry, Austin, Apr. 1, 1989). Her status as a special student is not confirmed, however, by Blanton's records in the University of Texas President's File.

30. University of Texas President's File for Annie Webb Blanton. The quote is from her 1924 Biographical Data Sheet in these files.
31. Thomas L. Blanton Vertical File, Barker Texas History Center; *Abilene Reporter-News,* Aug. 12, 1957; Bruce Lee Barney, "The Congressional Career of Thomas L. Blanton," Master's thesis, Hardin-Simmons University, 1966, pp. 1-2.
32. McDermott and Kilgore interview.
33. Blanton to Mrs. Percy V. (Anna) Pennybacker, Feb. 2, 1920, 2M27, Pennybacker Papers.
34. Dewey W. Grantham, *Southern Progressivism: The Reconciliation of Progress and Tradition,* pp. 246, 260, 270, 274, 415, 417-18; Joyce Antler, "The Educational Biography of Lucy Sprague Mitchell: A Case Study in the History of Women's Higher Education," p. 60, and Barbara Sicherman, "College and Careers: Historical Perspectives on the Lives and Work Patterns of Women College Graduates," p. 150, both in Faragher and Howe, eds., *Women and Higher Education.* Antler notes that classroom teaching has often been a terminal point for females and, conversely, a position from which to advance for males. Sicherman discusses the attitude that many women had concerning teaching as a career that offered no professional mobility *and* required a sacrifice in their personal life.

CHAPTER 2

1. Graham, "Expansion and Exclusion," pp. 761-62; Jessie Bernard, *Academic Women,* p. 32; Carter, "Academic Women Revisited," pp. 675-76; Linda L. Geary, *Balanced in the Wind: A Biography of Betsey Mix Cowles,* p. 86; Charles A. Harper, *A Century of Public Teacher Education,* pp. 72, 96-97. For a discussion of how women academics were directly affected by the broadening of higher education, see Geraldine Jonçich Clifford, ed., *Lone Voyagers: Academic Women in Coeducational Institutions, 1870-1937,* pp. 1-46.
2. Eby, *Development of Education,* pp. 294-95. According to Eby, Sam Houston began with a state legislative allotment of $14,000 plus a $6,000 donation from the Peabody Board. At the same time, the Prairie View Institute received $6,000 from the legislature for its operation. See also *Handbook of Texas,* 2:406. Prairie View was initially established in 1876 and opened in 1878 as Alta Vista Agricultural College, a branch of the Agricultural and Mechanical College of Texas for black students. When Alta Vista failed because of a lack of students, the legislature in 1879 mandated that the facility become Prairie View Normal School. This institution opened in 1885. (See Henry C. Dethloff, *A Centennial History*

of Texas A&M University, 1876–1976, 1:48, 54, 81, 311–14; *Handbook of Texas,* 2:406.)

3. George M. Crutsinger, *Survey Study of Teacher Training in Texas, and a Suggested Program,* pp. 12, 37–38; Paul K. Conkin, *Big Daddy from the Pedernales: Lyndon Baines Johnson,* pp. 39–40; Eby, *Development of Education,* pp. 294–97. Eby and Crutsinger give slightly different establishment dates for teacher training schools in San Marcos, Nacogdoches, and Alpine, but because Crutsinger's dates are based on primary source materials, I have used them.

4. Eby, *Development of Education,* pp. 295–96; *Handbook of Texas,* 2:287.

5. James L. Rogers, *The Story of North Texas from Texas Normal College, 1890, to North Texas State University, 1965,* pp. 5, 14, 26, 69; *Handbook of Texas,* 2:287; C. A. Bridges, *History of Denton, Texas from Its Beginning to 1960,* pp. 218, 222. From 1890 to 1990, North Texas has been known by these names: Texas Normal College, North Texas Normal College, North Texas State Normal College, North Texas State Teachers College, North Texas State College, North Texas State University, and the University of North Texas. (See *Handbook of Texas,* 2:287; Rogers, *Story,* pp. 23, 31, 88–89, 331–32, 348–50; Mike Kingston, ed., *1990–91 Texas Almanac and State Industrial Guide,* p. 527.)

6. Bridges, *History of Denton,* pp. 68–69, 212, 228, 250, 261, 263, 327; Rogers, *Story,* p. 122; Crutsinger, *Survey Study,* p. 12; interview with James L. Rogers, Denton, Feb. 13, 1987; Joyce Thompson, *Marking a Trail: A History of the Texas Woman's University,* pp. 3, 21.

7. Rogers, *Story,* pp. 46, 69, 122; Eby, *Development of Education,* p. 297; Bridges, *History of Denton,* p. 259. The quote is from Eby, p. 297.

8. Hill and Hill, *Isaac Hill,* pp. 44–47.

9. *Handbook of Texas,* 1:945–46; Rogers, *Story,* pp. 45–46; letter to me from Texas Education Agency, Sept. 18, 1986. National percentages for educational preparation of normal school faculty across the country in 1905 (four years after North Texas opened) were as follows: 25% held no degree, 46% held bachelor's degrees, 18% held master's degrees; 11% held doctoral degrees. At North Texas State Normal College in 1905, 41% held no degree; 12% held bachelor's degrees; 41% held master's degrees; 6% held doctoral degrees. (See Rogers, *Story,* p. 154.)

10. Rogers, *Story,* pp. 45–46; Cott, *Grounding,* p. 219; Lucille Addison Pollard, *Women on College and University Faculties: A Historical Survey and a Study of Their Present Academic Status;* Carter, "Academic Women Revisited," p. 680.

11. Graham, "Expansion and Exclusion," p. 766; Carter, "Academic

Women Revisited," pp. 679–80; Cott, *Grounding*, pp. 219, 221–22; Carol Ruth Berkin and Mary Beth Norton, *Women of America: A History*, pp. 319, 337–38.

12. Rogers, *Story*, pp. 159–64; *Handbook of Texas*, 1:229–30, 945–46; Blanton to W. H. Bruce, July 23, 1917, William H. Bruce File, University of North Texas Archives. Information on disagreements between Blanton and Bruce is found later in this chapter as well as in chapter 5.

13. Rogers, *Story*, pp. 45, 132; Rogers interview; *North Texas State Normal Journal* 2 (May, 1903): 56; Parker, *Annie Webb Blanton, Founder*, pp. 11–12; Holden, *Our Heritage*, 2:5–6; Jeanette Hastedt Flachmeier, *Pioneer Austin Notables*, 2:12–16; "Denton Woman One of Texas Leading Teachers," Annie Webb Blanton Vertical File; Megan Seaholm, "Earnest Women: The White Women's Club Movement in Progressive Era Texas, 1880–1920," Ph.D. diss., Rice University, 1988, pp. 238–39. Seaholm notes that in 1915, as part of the Shakespeare Club's participation in the presentation of the play *A Doll's House*, Blanton read a paper that she had written entitled "Woman's Duty to Herself," which may have been received skeptically by the other members. (See Seaholm, "Earnest Women," pp. 238–39; Feb. 25, 1915, Program, MSS8,3/6, Yearbooks, Woman's Shakespeare Club of Denton Files, The Woman's Collection, Texas Woman's University.) The living arrangement described here reflected the fact that women who pursued careers at this time usually were not married. (See Cott, *Grounding*, pp. 182–83; Kessler–Harris, *Out To Work*, p. 113.) In some ways, this arrangement is reminiscent of Jane Addams' shared living experience at Hull-House in Chicago. The obvious difference, of course, is that Blanton's decision to open her home to others was not meant to cross social class lines or to improve conditions of any lower-class groups. (See Jane Addams, *Twenty Years at Hull-House*, pp. 74, 76, 78–79, 89, 309.)

14. Delta Kappa Gamma, *Pioneer Women Teachers of Texas*, pp. 76–77; Parker, *Annie Webb Blanton, Founder*, p. 12; Blanton, *Hand Book*, p. 191; Blanton to Pennybacker, Feb. 13, 1916, Mar. 6, 1919, 2M53, Pennybacker Papers; Blanton to Pennybacker, Apr. 21, 1918, 2M124, Pennybacker Papers; *Campus Chat* 3 (Jan. 2, 1919), University of North Texas Archives; *Texas State Teachers' Association Bulletin* 2 (Feb., 1918): cover page. Blanton's interaction with men never moved beyond professional relationships. For example, another North Texas employee, W. E. James, also resigned his position to join her administration in 1918 as a rural school supervisor. James was a former student of Blanton's and had chaired her campaign committee in her race for state superintendent. But her relationship with him, unlike with Mitchell, was never more

than professional. (See *Campus Chat* 3 [Jan. 2, 1919]; "To Ex-Students of the North Texas State Normal College and to Personal Friends of Miss Annie Webb Blanton among the Teachers of Texas," Annie Webb Blanton Vertical File.)

15. Holden, *Our Heritage,* 1:19.

16. For a discussion on the significance of women's relationships with other women, see Blanche Wiesen Cook, "Female Support Networks and Political Activism: Lillian Wald, Crystal Eastman, Emma Goldman," in Nancy F. Cott and Elizabeth H. Pleck, eds., *A Heritage of Her Own: Toward a New Social History of American Women,* pp. 412–44; Leila J. Rupp, "'Imagine My Surprise': Women's Relationships in Historical Perspective," *Frontiers: A Journal of Women Studies* 5 (Fall, 1980): 61–70. In addition, *Frontiers* devoted its Fall, 1979, (vol. 4) edition to lesbian history; included is Lisa Duggan's helpful article "Lesbianism and American History: A Brief Source Review," pp. 80–85. For a discussion of "Boston marriages" see Susan Ware, *Beyond Suffrage: Women in the New Deal,* p. 26; Ware, *Partner and I;* Lillian Faderman, *Surpassing the Love of Men: Romantic Friendship and Love Between Women from the Renaissance to the Present,* pp. 190–203.

17. Rogers, *Story,* pp. 45, 156; North Texas State Teachers College Biographical Form, Completed by Annie Webb Blanton, 1927, Academic Affairs Office, University of North Texas; Blanton to Cooper, Mar. 6, 1929, Annie Webb Blanton Vertical File. Blanton's salary at the time of her departure in 1918 was approximately $2,000 per year. (See Blanton to William Seneca Sutton, June 15, 1923, HQ340, William Seneca Sutton Papers, Barker Texas History Center.)

18. *North Texas State Normal Journal* 2 (May, 1903): 56; Rogers, *Story,* p. 131; Parker, *Annie Webb Blanton, Founder,* pp. 10–11; Blanton to Pennybacker, Apr. 24, 1918, 2M124, Pennybacker Papers.

19. Rogers, *Story,* p. 122; *The Yucca* 2 (1908), University of North Texas Archives.

20. Blanton to Bruce, July 23, 1917, Bruce File. Blanton's correspondence to Bruce resulted from his indication to English faculty members in 1917 that the North Texas curriculum included too much emphasis on technical grammar. Blanton took this as a personal affront and responded with two detailed and dramatic letters in which she defended the need for grammar instruction and noted its comparable nature to courses taught at more prestigious schools, such as the University of Texas, as well as other normal schools. In her correspondence Blanton clearly expressed respectful impatience with Bruce's attitude and his failure to grasp details she believed to be important. She noted

that, "If these courses must be constantly defended from attack, it is my preference that they be discontinued." However, she added, "In twenty-one courses, which we offer in all, four on the structure of the language does not seem obsessive." (See also Blanton to Bruce, July 26, 1917, Bruce File.)

21. Rogers, *Story,* p. 158; Blanton to Cooper, Mar. 6, 1929, Annie Webb Blanton Vertical File; Biographical Data Sheets, University of Texas President's File for Annie Webb Blanton; Annie Webb Blanton, *Review Outline and Exercises in English Grammar;* Blanton, *Supplemental Exercises in Punctuation and Composition.* On her biographical data sheets, Blanton listed the dates of publication for these books (often with slightly different titles) variously from 1908 to 1910. I have been able to locate copies only of *Review Outline* (at Delta Kappa Gamma International Headquarters, Austin) and *Supplemental Exercises* (at Barker Texas History Center), both with 1909 publication dates. *Review Outline* has a 1909 revised date but lists no initial date of publication. It does not appear that Blanton ever used her own books exclusively in her classes at North Texas. (See Blanton to Bruce, July 23, 1917, Bruce File.)

22. Blanton to Bruce, July 23, 1917, Bruce File; North Texas State Teachers College Biographical Form; Blanton to Sutton, June 15, 1923, HQ340, Sutton Papers; Faculty of the Graduate School Membership Blank, University of Texas President's File for Annie Webb Blanton.

23. *Denton Record-Chronicle,* July 29, 1918; Blanton to Pennybacker, Sept. 15, 1917, 2M52, Pennybacker Papers; Pennybacker to F. M. Bralley, Nov. 27, 1917, 2M52, Pennybacker Papers.

24. Holden, *Our Heritage,* 2:15; *Campus Chat* 1 (Apr. 5, 1917); 1 (July 19, 1917); *Texas State Teachers' Association Bulletin* 3 (Mar., 1919): 77. Bruce joined the first faculty of North Texas in 1901 as a math professor and was president of the school from 1906 to 1923. He served as TSTA president in 1905. (See Rogers, *Story,* pp. 159–64.)

25. Blanton to Pennybacker, Sept. 15, 1917, 2M52, Pennybacker Papers; "Annie Webb Blanton Memorial Resolution," Annie Webb Blanton Vertical File.

26. Texas State Teachers Association Vertical File, Barker Texas History Center; *Handbook of Texas,* 2:764, 3:997; *Texas State Teachers' Association Bulletin* 1 (Feb., 1917): 82–85; Junior Nathaniel Nelum, "A Study of the First Seventy Years of the Colored Teachers State Association of Texas," Ph.D. diss., University of Texas, Austin, 1955, pp. 21–22; Calvert and De León, *History,* pp. 239, 261; Vernon McDaniel, *The History of the Teachers State Association of Texas,* pp. 78, 161–62. In 1917, some 2,800 teachers were TSTA members, which was about 10% of the education

profession in Texas. (See "Denton Woman One of Texas Leading Educators," Annie Webb Blanton Vertical File.)

27. Blanton to Pennybacker, Sept. 15, 1917, 2M52, Pennybacker Papers.

28. *Texas State Teachers' Association Bulletin* 1 (Feb., 1917): 84.

29. Ibid.

30. *Denton Record-Chronicle*, Dec. 12, 1916.

31. *Texas State Teachers' Association Bulletin* 1 (Feb., 1917): 83–85. The other female nominated was Mrs. Maggie W. Barry of Sherman.

32. Ibid., p. 84.

33. *Texas State Teachers' Association Bulletin* 1 (Feb., 1917): 85; *Denton Record-Chronicle*, Dec. 2, 1916.

34. *Texas School Journal* 34 (Dec., 1916): 14.

35. Blanton to Cooper, Mar. 6, 1929, Annie Webb Blanton Vertical File. Arnie Weissman, in "Annie Webb Blanton," *Texas Outlook* 65 (Winter, 1981–82): 21, wrote that Blanton lobbied the state prior to her election.

36. *Denton Record-Chronicle*, Dec. 4, 1916.

37. Berry interview; Blanton to Pennybacker, May 6, 1918, 2M124, Pennybacker Papers; "A Tribute to Dr. Annie Webb Blanton," Blanton Biographical File.

38. *Denton Record-Chronicle*, Dec. 4, 1916.

39. Ibid., Dec. 5, 1916.

40. *Texas State Teachers' Association Bulletin* 2 (Feb., 1918): 7.

41. Ibid.

42. Blanton to Pennybacker, Apr. 4, 1917, 2M52, Pennybacker Papers.

43. Blanton to Cooper, Mar. 6, 1929, Annie Webb Blanton Vertical File.

44. Ibid.; Blanton to Mrs. R. H. Garrison, Apr. 11, 1917, MSS8, 1/1, Correspondence, Woman's Shakespeare Club of Denton Files; "Why Texas Teachers Should Support Annie Webb Blanton for State Superintendent of Public Instruction," Campaign Handbill, Annie Webb Blanton Vertical File. Blanton's year in office coincided with Governor Ferguson's battle with the University of Texas and his subsequent resignation from office, but no substantial evidence of Blanton's reaction to these events in her role as president was located. Blanton's individual reaction to Ferguson is discussed in chapter 3.

45. *Texas State Teachers' Association Bulletin* 1 (Oct., 1917): 41; 2 (Feb., 1918): 13–15, 27–29. Young was also the first woman president of the National Education Association, elected in 1910. (See Allan M. West, *The National Education Association: The Power Base for Education*, p. 24.)

46. Blanton to Pennybacker, Sept. 15, 1917, 2M52, Pennybacker Papers.

47. *Texas State Teachers' Association Bulletin* 1 (Oct., 1917): 41; 2 (Feb., 1918): 13–15, 27–29.

48. Blanton to Cunningham, Dec. 25, 1917, MS74, 15/225, Cunningham Papers.

49. *Texas State Teachers' Association Bulletin* 2 (Feb., 1918): 6–7. The theme of democracy in education was often employed by southern Pro.gressives, commonly with Jeffersonian references. Significantly, Jefferson's concerns had addressed education only for white people. (See Grantham, *Southern Progressivism*, p. 256; Merrill D. Peterson, *The Jefferson Image in the American Mind*, pp. 240–41; Anderson, *Education*, p. 1.)

50. *Texas State Teachers' Association Bulletin* 2 (Feb., 1918): 6, 57–58; letter to me from Texas State Teachers Association, Apr. 26, 1989.

51. *Texas State Teachers' Association Bulletin* 2 (Feb., 1918): 57–58; Murray interview.

52. *Texas School Journal* 83 (Jan., 1921): 10–12; letter to me from Texas State Teachers Association, Apr. 26, 1989. Williams later joined Blanton as a founder of Delta Kappa Gamma, as discussed in chapter 5.

53. *Texas State Teachers' Association Bulletin* 1 (Oct., 1917): 3; 3 (Mar., 1919): 29; Blanton to Pennybacker, Dec. 4, 1917, 2M52, Pennybacker Papers; *Texas School Journal* 38 (Dec., 1920): 15–16, 20; 38 (Jan., 1921): 10–13.

54. Winegarten, *Texas Women*, p. 100; *Texas School Journal* 35 (Nov., 1917): 18; Anna J. Hardwicke Pennybacker, *A New History of Texas for Schools;* "The Conference for Education in Texas: Declaration of Principles and Policies," 2M124, Pennybacker Papers; Lee Clark to Pennybacker, July 15, 1912, 2M45, Pennybacker Papers.

55. Annie Webb Blanton to William Seneca Sutton, Feb. 17, 1907, 4J279, Conference for Education in Texas Records, Barker Texas History Center (quote); Phonsie Campbell, "William Seneca Sutton," Master's thesis, University of Texas, Austin, 1932, pp. 67, 79; Grantham, *Southern Progressivism*, pp. 67–79. The larger educational reform movement in the South began in 1898 with the Conference for Education in the South, a group that initially brought northern philanthropists and southern white education reformers together to discuss, among other issues, the education of blacks. The group held conferences each year and eventually established both the Southern Education Board and the General Education Board. The exact reasons for Texas not participating directly in the Conference for Education in the South are

not clear, although the larger movement's emphasis on resolving black education and its strong southeastern representation may have been contributing factors. (See Grantham, *Southern Progressivism*, p. 247; Anderson, *Education*, pp. 83–87.)

56. Winegarten, *Texas Women*, p. 100; Pennybacker to Blanton, Jan. 16, 1915, 2M103, Pennybacker Papers; Blanton to Pennybacker, Sept. 15, Oct. 26, 1917, 2M52, Pennybacker Papers; William P. Hobby to Blanton, Sept. 19, Oct. 15, 25, 30, 1917, William P. Hobby Papers, Archives Division, Texas State Library.

57. Blanton to Pennybacker, Jan. 19, Apr. 3, 10, 1918, 2M124, Pennybacker Papers.

58. Grantham, *Southern Progressivism*, pp. 207, 415, 417–18.

59. *The Alcalde* 6 (Feb., 1918): 292.

60. Blanton to Pennybacker, Apr. 21, 24, May 6, 1918, 2M124, Pennybacker Papers; Blanton to Pennybacker, May 14, 1918, 2M57, Pennybacker Papers.

61. Blanton to Pennybacker, May 6, 1918, 2M124, Pennybacker Papers.

62. Blanton to Pennybacker, June 17, 27, 1918, 2M57, Pennybacker Papers; Blanton to Pennybacker, Aug. 9, 1918, 2M47, Pennybacker Papers; Judie Walton Gammage, "Quest for Equality: An Historical Overview of Women's Rights Activism in Texas, 1890–1975," Ph.D. diss., University of North Texas, 1982, pp. 42–43.

63. Blanton to Pennybacker, Oct. 22, 1918, 2M47, Pennybacker Papers; various letters between Blanton and Pennybacker, Oct. 28, 1918–Sept. 6, 1919, 2M36, 2M47, 2M48, 2M53, 2M56, Pennybacker Papers. Household concerns ranged from maintenance of the water pipes to relationships with black servants. Correspondence between the two after the fall of 1919 is found in the Pennybacker Papers, boxes 2M6, 2M20, 2M22, 2M26, 2M27, 2M28, 2M29, 2M31, 2M34, 2M35, 2M36, 2M37, 2M51, 2M53, 2M54, 2M57, 2M58, 2M59, 2M78, 2M80, 2M84, 2M96. When Pennybacker died in 1938, Blanton was listed among those who sent flowers. (See 2M119, Pennybacker Papers.)

64. See, for example, letters previously cited in Pennybacker collection as compared to correspondence between Blanton and Pittenger in 4R26, Benjamin F. Pittenger Papers, Barker Texas History Center.

65. The vice presidency of the National Education Association was usually held by ten to twelve members simultaneously and was as much ceremonial as substantive. But Blanton did make several speeches before the group, and earned some recognition at the group's 1920 meeting in Salt Lake City when she temporarily chaired the resolutions

committee and introduced a resolution that called for immediate action on the federal suffrage amendment by those states that had not yet ratified it. Her service also put her in closer contact with Colorado state superintendent Mary C. C. Bradford, who served as National Education Association president in 1917–18. (See Faculty of the Graduate School Membership Blank, University of Texas President's File for Annie Webb Blanton; *Denton Record-Chronicle,* July 8, 1920; *The Journal of the National Education Association* 10 [Mar., 1921]: 61; *National Education Association Bulletin* 8 [Sept., 1919]: 2; 4 [Sept., 1917]: 2, 14–15.)

66. Rogers, *Story,* pp. 69, 84; Legislative Committee to Investigate State Departments and Institutions, 1917, Subcommittee No. 10, 2–8/527, 263–348, Archives Division, Texas State Library. As state superintendent, Blanton placed the Texas normal colleges on the accredited college list late in 1919.

67. Rogers, *Story,* pp. 45, 158, 164; Legislative Committee to Investigate State Departments and Institutions, 1917.

68. *Denton Record-Chronicle,* Sept. 14, 1918.

CHAPTER 3

1. *Denton Record-Chronicle,* July 28, 29, 1918; Blanton to Cooper, Mar. 6, 1929, Annie Webb Blanton Vertical File.

2. Winegarten and McArthur, *Citizens,* pp. 165, 172.

3. "Address of Miss Annie Webb Blanton," July 1918, MS74, 15/226, Cunningham Papers; *Texas School Journal* 32 (Apr., 1915): 19.

4. Blanton to Pennybacker, May 10, 1918, 2M124, Pennybacker Papers; Blanton to Cunningham, Mar. 20, May 10, 1918, MS74, 15/225, Cunningham Papers; Grantham, *Southern Progressivism,* pp. 274, 410; Lewis L. Gould, *Progressives and Prohibitionists: Texas Democrats in the Wilson Era,* p. xiii.

5. Gould, *Progressives and Prohibitionists,* pp. 188, 190–95, 199, 205, 215–18, 228.

6. Ibid., pp. 232–35.

7. Grantham, *Southern Progressivism,* pp. xv–xvi, 207, 212, 213, 216, 415, 417–18; Anne Firor Scott and Andrew MacKay Scott, *One Half the People: The Fight for Woman Suffrage,* pp. 66–68.

8. Winegarten and McArthur, *Citizens,* pp. 13, 26–27, 34–38, 202–12. In a paper entitled "Democrats Divided: Why the Texas Legislature Gave Women Primary Suffrage in 1918" and given at the 1991 Southern Historical Association meeting McArthur presented evidence showing that the attainment of primary suffrage in Texas, a state with no particularly strong suffrage support in the state legislature or elsewhere,

resulted from Minnie Fisher Cunningham's exploitation of political circumstances. Despite legislators and suffragists claiming that women's voting rights were granted in Texas as reward for the women's good and faithful work on behalf of the war, it is clear that the real reason for the success of the primary suffrage bill rested with Cunningham's promise to progressive members of the Democratic Party, eager to keep Ferguson out of office, that she would deliver the votes of women for Hobby if a primary suffrage bill was considered in the special legislative session.

9. Winegarten and McArthur, *Citizens,* pp. 172, 213–14; *Austin American,* Mar. 21, June 29, 1918; *Dallas Morning News,* July 11, 1918; *Houston Post,* July 4, 9, 12, 1918; *Farm and Ranch,* Apr. 6, 1918. I appreciate Judith N. McArthur sharing her information on black women with me, presented initially in her paper "Gender Politics: Women Voters and the Texas Primary of 1918," given at the 1991 conference of the Southern Association of Women Historians.

10. Winegarten and McArthur, *Citizens,* p. 37 (quote); Gould, *Progressives and Prohibitionists,* pp. 236, 241.

11. Blanton to Helen Moore, Apr. 24, 1918, MS74, 15/225, Cunningham Papers; Blanton to Pennybacker, Apr. 3, 1918, 2M124, Pennybacker Papers; Blanton to Cooper, Mar. 6, 1929, Annie Webb Blanton Vertical File; University of Texas President's File for Annie Webb Blanton; Employment Records of Annie Webb Blanton, Austin Independent School District; Rogers, *Story,* p. 159; *Texas State Teachers' Association Bulletin* 1 (Feb., 1917): 83; *Texas School Journal* 34 (Dec., 1916): 14. The Texas Congress of Mothers also was known as the State Congress of Mothers and then, later, the Texas Congress of Parents and Teachers, which is today commonly called the Parent-Teachers Association or PTA. (See Eby, *Development of Education,* p. 236; *Handbook of Texas,* 2:737, 3:975; Kingston, *1990–91 Texas Almanac,* p. 534.)

12. Blanton to Cunningham, Mar. 11, 1918, MS74, 15/225, Cunningham Papers.

13. Blanton to Cunningham, May 10, 1918, MS74, 15/225, Cunningham Papers; Blanton to Pennybacker, Apr. 21, 1918, 2M124, Pennybacker Papers.

14. Gould, *Progressives and Prohibitionists,* pp. 186–87; *Texas School Journal* 32 (Feb., 1915): 17; "Address of Miss Annie Webb Blanton," July 1918, MS74, 15/226, Cunningham Papers; *State Topics and the Texas Monthly Review* 10 (June, 1918): 14.

15. *Denton Record-Chronicle,* June 18, 1918; Blanton to A. C. Allison, July 7, 1918, MS74, 15/226, Cunningham Papers.

16. Blanton to Pennybacker, Apr. 24, 1918, 2M124, Pennybacker Papers; Blanton to Cunningham, June 19, 1918, MS74, 15/225, Cunningham Papers.
17. Blanton to Pennybacker, Oct. 22, 1918, 2M47, Pennybacker Papers.
18. Blanton to Cunningham, Aug. 14, 1917, MS74, 15/225, Cunningham Papers.
19. Aileen S. Kraditor, *The Ideas of the Woman Suffrage Movement, 1890–1920,* pp. 44, 52.
20. Blanton to Cunningham, Dec. 25, 1917, Mar. 20, 1918, MS74, 15/225, Cunningham Papers.
21. Blanton to Cunningham, Mar. 20, 1918, MS74, 15/225, Cunningham Papers.
22. *Denton Record-Chronicle,* May 25, 1918.
23. Blanton to Pennybacker, May 11, 1919, 2M56, Pennybacker Papers.
24. Arthur S. Link and Richard L. McCormick, *Progressivism,* p. 56; Grantham, *Southern Progressivism,* pp. 212, 216.
25. "Annie Webb Blanton for State Superintendent of Public Instruction," Broadside, Annie Webb Blanton Vertical File; MSS32, Texas Federation of Women's Clubs Files, The Woman's Collection, Texas Woman's University; *Texas School Journal* 37 (Sept., 1919): 9–10; Humphrey, *A Texas Suffragist,* p. 65; Kraditor, *Ideas,* p. 252; McDermott and Kilgore interview; interview with Kay Goad (a cousin of Blanton's), Euless, July 14, 1988. As noted in chapter 2, Cunningham and Pennybacker did not hold each other in close regard, primarily because Cunningham believed that Pennybacker had been slow to support the suffrage cause initially, yet had been recognized by national suffrage groups later as if she had been a significant leader early in the movement. This tension, however, did not seem to affect the relationship that Blanton had with each of these women, and there is no evidence that they discussed their feelings about one another with Blanton.
26. Rogers, *Story,* pp. 46, 105; Blanton to Cooper, Mar. 6, 1929, Annie Webb Blanton Vertical File.
27. *Texas School Journal* 37 (Oct., 1919): 9.
28. Cott, *Grounding,* pp. 271, 283; "Annie Webb Blanton for State Superintendent of Public Instruction," Broadside, Annie Webb Blanton Vertical File; McDermott and Kilgore interview; Goad interview.
29. Anne Firor Scott, "The 'New Woman' in the New South," *South Atlantic Quarterly* 61 (Autumn, 1962): 473–83; Cott, *Grounding,* p. 231; Anne

Firor Scott, *The Southern Lady: From Pedestal to Politics, 1830–1930,* pp. 208, 220; Grantham, *Southern Progressivism,* pp. 202–204.

30. Blanton to Pennybacker, Apr. 3, 21, 1918, 2M124, Pennybacker Papers; Horowitz, *Alma Mater,* p. 193. For an account of the viewpoint that female teachers would have a positive impact as voters, see Alice Stone Blackwell, "Do Teachers Need the Ballot?" *Journal of Education* 70 (July 1, 1909): 8–9.

31. Blanton to Edith Hinkle League, Jan. 2, 1917, MS74, 15/225, Cunningham Papers; Blanton to Cunningham, Aug. 14, Nov. 23, 1917, MS74, 15/225, Cunningham Papers.

32. Blanton to Cunningham, Mar. 11, 1918, MS74, 15/225, Cunningham Papers.

33. Blanton to Pennybacker, Apr. 3, 21, 1918, 2M124, Pennybacker Papers.

34. Blanton to Cunningham, May 5, 10, June 10, 1918, MS74, 15/225, Cunningham Papers; Blanton to Moore, Apr. 24, 1918, MS74, 15/225, Cunningham Papers; Blanton to Pennybacker, Apr. 10, 24, May 6, 1918, 2M124, Pennybacker Papers.

35. Blanton to Cunningham, May 10, 1918, MS74, 15/225, Cunningham Papers.

36. Cunningham to C. B. Metcalfe, Feb. 13, 1918, MS74, 14/23, Cunningham Papers. See note 8 above.

37. Mary H. Ellis to Blanton, Jan. 2, 1919, 4/7, Jane Y. McCallum Papers, Austin History Center (quote); Cunningham to Blanton, May 23, 1918, MS74, 15/225, Cunningham Papers; Thomas L. Blanton to Cunningham, Jan. 28, May 26, 1917, MS74, 14/202, Cunningham Papers; Blanton to Pennybacker, Sept. 15, 1917, 2M52, Pennybacker Papers; Blanton to Pennybacker, May 10, 1918, 2M124, Pennybacker Papers; *Texas School Journal* 37 (June, 1920): 12. Utah also had had a female state superintendent who served an appointed term for three months in 1900 following the death of the incumbent. (See Carol Ann Lubomudrov, "A Woman State School Superintendent: Whatever Happened to Mrs. McVicker?" *Utah Historical Quarterly* 49 [Summer, 1989]: 254–61.)

38. *Austin American,* June 1, 1918; *Denton Record-Chronicle,* June 1, 3, 1918.

39. Blanton to Pennybacker, Feb. 2, 1920, 2M27, Pennybacker Papers.

40. Grantham, *Southern Progressivism,* pp. xv–xxii, 34, 256–57; Gould, *Progressives and Prohibitionists,* p. 289; Holden, *Our Heritage,* 2:11–12.

41. *Handbook of Texas,* 1:516; letter to me from Texas Education Agency, Sept. 18, 1986.

42. *State Topics and the Texas Monthly Review* 10 (June, 1918): 14; *Texas School Journal* 35 (Dec., 1917): 12, 34.

43. Anti-Saloon League, *The Brewers and Texas Politics*, 1:1–2.

44. Cunningham to W. F. Doughty, June 10, 1918, MS74, 15/226, Cunningham Papers (quote); "Shall the Fathers and Mothers of Texas or the Brewers and German-American Alliance O.K. Our State Superintendent of Public Instruction?" Campaign Brochure, MS74, 15/226, Cunningham Papers; Undated Newspaper Clipping, 2P363, Alexander Caswell Ellis Papers, Barker Texas History Center; *Austin Statesman*, July 21, 1918; Gould, *Progressives and Prohibitionists*, pp. 239, 301; "Doughty States Facts About the Correspondence Between Him and a Former Member of the Texas Legislature," Campaign Letter, HQ330, Sutton Papers.

45. Cunningham to Doughty, June 10, 1918, MS74, 15/226, Cunningham Papers.

46. Alexander Caswell Ellis to Cunningham, July 10, 1918, MS74, 15/226, Cunningham Papers.

47. Gould, *Progressives and Prohibitionists*, pp. 193, 208; Lewis L. Gould, "The University Becomes Politicized: The War with Jim Ferguson, 1915–1918," *Southwestern Historical Quarterly* 86 (Oct., 1982): 265, 274; Alexander Caswell Ellis Vertical File, Barker Texas History Center.

48. Ellis to Cunningham, June 20, July 7, 1918, MS74, 15/226, Cunningham Papers.

49. Ellis to Cunningham, July 2, 8, 1918, MS74, 15/226, Cunningham Papers; Cunningham to Blanton, July 9, 1918, MS74, 15/226, Cunningham Papers.

50. Ellis to Cunningham, June 20, 1918, MS74, 15/226, Cunningham Papers.

51. Ellis to Cunningham, July 10, 1918, MS74, 15/226, Cunningham Papers.

52. Blanton to Cunningham, June 21, July 15, 16, 1918, MS74, 15/225, Cunningham Papers; *Denton Record-Chronicle*, June 14, 17, 1918.

53. "Miss Blanton Corrects False Statements," Campaign Brochure, Annie Webb Blanton Vertical File; Blanton to Pennybacker, Aug. 9, 1918, 2M47, Pennybacker Papers.

54. "Address of Miss Annie Webb Blanton," July 1918, MS74, 15/226, Cunningham Papers; *Denton Record-Chronicle*, June 18, 1918; Blanton to Cunningham, June 21, 1918, MS74, 15/225, Cunningham Papers; "Vote for Annie Webb Blanton," Campaign Brochure, MS74, 15/225, Cunningham Papers.

55. Doughty to Cunningham, June 7, 1918, MS74, 15/226, Cunning-

ham Papers; Ellis to Cunningham, July 19, 1918, MS74, 15/226, Cunningham Papers; Blanton to Pennybacker, Aug. 9, 1918, 2M47, Pennybacker Papers; *Austin Statesman,* July 21, 1918; *Austin American,* July 21, 1918; *Denton Record-Chronicle,* June 26, July 24, 1918; "Concerning the Race for State Superintendent of Public Instruction," "Miss Blanton Corrects False Statements," Campaign Brochures, Annie Webb Blanton Vertical File; "Doughty States Facts," Campaign Letter, HQ330, Sutton Papers; "Miss Blanton Explains Doughty's Endorsement," Undated Newspaper Advertisement, William Seneca Sutton Vertical File, Barker Texas History Center. It is interesting that much contemporary research on Blanton, for example the exhibit on Texas women on permanent display at Texas Woman's University in Denton, has portrayed Doughty's effort in his 1918 race as a "smear campaign" against Blanton, an oversimplification that does not recognize that Blanton and her supporters were the more aggressive campaigners.

56. Doughty to the Friends of Education, HQ330, Sutton Papers; "Doughty's Record," Campaign Brochure, 4Q333, Sutton Papers; Blanton to Cunningham, Aug. 21, 1918, MS74, 15/225, Cunningham Papers; *State Topics and the Texas Monthly Review* 10 (June, 1918): 14.

57. "Shall the Fathers and Mothers of Texas or the Brewers and German-American Alliance O.K. Our State Superintendent of Public Instruction?" Campaign Brochure, MS74, 15/226, Cunningham Papers.

58. *Denton Record-Chronicle,* Aug. 13, 1918; *Dallas Morning News,* July 30, 1918; Blanton to Cooper, Mar. 6, 1929, Annie Webb Blanton Vertical File; Gould, *Progressives and Prohibitionists,* p. 245; Winegarten and McArthur, *Citizens,* p. 172; *New York Times,* July 29, 1918.

59. *Texas School Journal* 36 (Sept., 1918): 18.

60. Ibid. 32 (Apr., 1915): 9, 14, 19, 21; Grantham, *Southern Progressivism,* pp. 14, 246–47, 253; Eby, *Development of Education,* pp. 230–31; Anderson, *Education,* pp. 82–87.

61. *Public Schools Laws of the State of Texas,* pp. 13–17; Grantham, *Southern Progressivism,* p. 257.

62. *Denton Record-Chronicle,* July 29, 31, 1918; Blanton to Pennybacker, Oct. 22, 1918, 2M47, Pennybacker Papers; Blanton to Pennybacker, June 11, 1919, 2M36, Pennybacker Papers.

63. *Texas School Journal* 36 (Feb., 1919): 9; 37 (Sept., 1919): 9–10; Blanton to Pennybacker, Oct. 22, 1918, 2M47, Pennybacker Papers; Blanton to Pennybacker, Dec. 2, 1918, 2M48, Pennybacker Papers; Blanton to Pennybacker, June 11, 1919, 2M36, Pennybacker Papers.

64. *Texas School Journal* 37 (Oct., 1919): 9.

65. For a discussion of *"Herrenvolk* democracy" (democracy for whites only), see Grantham, *Southern Progressivism,* pp. xvii, 118.
66. *Texas School Journal* 37 (Oct., 1919): 9.
67. *Dallas Times Herald,* Jan. 21, 1923; Blanton, *Hand Book,* pp. 57–58. Blanton did draw the ire of her former boss, W. H. Bruce, over her determination that the State Department of Education become directly involved in visiting and making suggestions for improvements to teachers in service. This role previously had been carried out solely by teacher training schools and departments, and Bruce resented Blanton's broadening of the responsibilities of the Department of Education. This disagreement, however, did not focus on opportunities for women and seems to have been no more than a difference of opinion on policy. (See Bruce to Blanton, Aug. 21, 1919, Bruce File.)
68. Blanton, *Hand Book,* p. 59.
69. *Texas School Journal* 38 (Dec., 1920): 14–15; *Dallas Times Herald,* Jan. 21, 1923; "Annie Webb Blanton of Denton," Handbill, University of North Texas Archives.
70. *Texas School Journal* 36 (Sept., 1918): 18.
71. *Dallas Times Herald,* Jan. 21, 1923; Blanton, *Hand Book.*
72. *Texas School Journal* 37 (Jan., 1920): 11.
73. *Texas School Journal* 37 (Sept., 1919): 11; (Jan., 1920): 11; (Feb., 1920): 10, 27; Blanton to Cooper, Mar. 6, 1929, Annie Webb Blanton Vertical File; Blanton to Pennybacker, Aug. 4, 1919, 2M36, Pennybacker Papers; Blanton, *Hand Book;* Grantham, *Southern Progressivism,* p. 261; *Dallas Times Herald,* Jan. 21, 1923; Eby, *Development of Education,* pp. 230–31; C. E. Evans, *The Story of Texas Schools,* p. 126; Emma Louise Moyer Jackson, "Petticoat Politics: Political Activism Among Texas Women in the 1920s," Ph.D. diss., University of Texas, Austin, 1980, pp. 193, 205–206.
74. Blanton to Allison, July 7, 1918, MS74, 15/226, Cunningham Papers; Blanton to Cooper, Mar. 6, 1929, Annie Webb Blanton Vertical File.
75. Annie Webb Blanton, "A Study of Educational Progress in Texas, 1918–1922," Master's thesis, University of Texas, Austin, 1923, p. 320.
76. Blanton, *Hand Book,* p. 29.
77. Blanton to Cooper, Mar. 6, 1929, Annie Webb Blanton Vertical File; Blanton, *Hand Book.*
78. *Texas School Journal* 38 (Sept., 1920): 9; Better Schools Campaign Materials, Frederick Eby Papers, Texas Collection, Baylor University; Eby, *Development of Education,* p. 234; Evans, *Story,* p. 125.
79. *Texas School Journal* 37 (Jan., 1920): 11.
80. *Dallas Morning News,* Nov. 2, 1920; *Texas School Journal* 37 (Jan.,

1920): 11; Eby, *Development of Education,* p. 234; Better Schools Campaign Materials, Eby Papers; Evans, *Story,* p. 125; Irving Owen Dawson, "The Texas State Teachers Association: A Study in Public Employee Organization," Ph.D. diss., University of Texas, Austin, 1958, pp. 327–31.

81. Eby, *Development of Education,* p. 234.

82. *Texas School Journal* 38 (Dec., 1920): 14–15; (Feb., 1921): 9, 12.

83. Blanton to Cooper, Mar. 6, 1929, Annie Webb Blanton Vertical File.

84. Jackson, "Petticoat Politics," pp. 193–97.

85. Blanton to Cooper, Mar. 6, 1929, Annie Webb Blanton Vertical File (quote); *Texas School Journal* 38 (Dec., 1920): 14–15; 38 (Feb., 1921): 12.

86. Grantham, *Southern Progressivism,* pp. 247, 253; *Texas School Journal* 36 (Jan., 1919): 20; Blanton to Cooper, Mar. 6, 1929, Annie Webb Blanton Vertical File.

87. Blanton to Pennybacker, June 11, 1919, 2M36, Pennybacker Papers; "Annie Webb Blanton of Denton," Political Handbills File, University of North Texas Archives.

88. *Texas School Journal* 39 (Feb., 1922): 15; Starlin Marion Newberry Marrs Vertical File, Barker Texas History Center; Blanton to W. C. Hogg, June 24, 1922, William Clifford Hogg Papers, Barker Texas History Center; "Ed. R. Bentley," Campaign Brochure, HQ330, Sutton Papers; Norman D. Brown, *Hood, Bonnet, and Little Brown Jug: Texas Politics, 1921–1928,* pp. 110, 117. As a normal school graduate, Bentley probably believed Blanton's certificate revisions were too intrusive to teacher training schools. This issue is discussed further in chapter 4.

89. *Denton Record-Chronicle,* Mar. 16, 20, Apr. 5, 1922.

90. *Denton Record-Chronicle,* Mar. 16, 28, 29, Apr. 3, 4, 5, 1922; *Texas School Journal* 39 (Apr., 1922): 11. At least one other Texas woman ran for Congress in 1922. Fannie May Barbee Hughs of Wharton County lost in her bid for the ninth district seat. (See *Wharton Spectator,* July 21, 29, Aug. 4, 1922.)

91. *Denton Record-Chronicle,* Apr. 13 (quote), 14, 1922; "Annie Webb Blanton of Denton," Political Handbills File, University of North Texas Archives; "Annie Webb Blanton, Democratic Candidate for Representative in Congress," Handbill, 2M78, Pennybacker Papers. Blanton's attitude toward the Klan was similar to that of many Progressives in Texas. For example, attorney Thomas B. Love, leader of Woodrow Wilson's forces in Texas and longtime prominent Progressive, believed the group was misguided but nevertheless moral. In the 1924 governor's race, Love supported Klan candidate Felix D. Robertson over Miriam A. Ferguson because of the Klan's dry stance. (See Evan Anders, "Thomas

Watt Gregory and the Survival of His Progressive Faith," *Southwestern Historical Quarterly* 93 [July, 1989]: 11–12; Calvert and De León, *History,* p. 286.)

92. *Denton Record-Chronicle,* Apr. 6, 1922; Barney, "The Congressional Career of Thomas L. Blanton," p. 25; Seth Shepard McKay, *Texas Politics 1906–1944, with Special Reference to the German Counties,* p. 167. Blanton had caused a previous uproar in 1921 over a speech which his colleagues considered to be too indecent for inclusion in the *Congressional Record.* The result of that episode was an attempt to remove him from Congress, which failed, and a successful vote to censure him. (See Thomas L. Blanton Vertical File; "Off the Record," Aug. 21–27, 1989, *Washington Post National Weekly Edition,* p. 33.)

93. U.S. Congress, House of Representatives, *Congressional Record,* 67th Cong., 2d sess. (Mar. 23 to Apr. 12, 1922) 62, 5:5120.

94. *Denton Record-Chronicle,* Apr. 8, 24, 1922; Blanton to G. W. Barcus, Aug. 23, 1920, Travis County File, Pat Neff Papers, Texas Collection, Baylor University.

95. *Denton Record-Chronicle,* Apr. 14, 28, May 3, 15, 1922; *Dallas Morning News,* May 14, 1922; *Handbook of Texas,* 2:912. Ironically, Tom Blanton went on to succeed in his own bid for reelection to Congress in 1922 by using his strong support for woman suffrage as a campaign issue. (See Barney, "The Congressional Career of Thomas L. Blanton," pp. 79–80.)

96. *Denton Record-Chronicle,* Apr. 11, 1922; Mrs. E. D. Criddle to Pennybacker, May 6, 1922, Pennybacker Papers.

97. *Denton Record-Chronicle,* May 16, 1922.

98. *Dallas Morning News,* May 18, 1922.

99. Blanton to Pennybacker, May 31, 1922, 2M80, Pennybacker Papers (quote); Cott, *Grounding,* pp. 271, 277–78; *Dallas Morning News,* May 16, 1922.

100. *Texas School Journal* 40 (Jan., 1923): 7; 41 (Sept., 1923): 8.

101. *Texas School Journal* 41 (Sept., 1923): 8; letter to me from Texas Education Agency, Sept. 18, 1986; Hope Chamberlain, *A Minority of Members: Women in the U.S. Congress,* pp. 315–16. The office of state superintendent was renamed commissioner of education and made an appointive office in 1951. Through 1991, no female has been appointed to this position. Miriam Ferguson, the wife of former governor James E. Ferguson, served as governor of Texas from 1925 to 1927 and 1933 to 1935. Ann Richards was elected to serve as state treasurer from 1983 to 1991; in 1991 she began her term as governor. Also in 1991, Kay Bailey Hutchison began her elective term as state treasurer. (See

Kingston, *1990–91 Texas Almanac,* pp. 361, 435; *Dallas Morning News,* Mar. 2, 3, 1991.)

CHAPTER 4

1. "To the Women of Texas," Apr. 22, 1922, 2M78, Pennybacker Papers; Blanton to Cooper, Mar. 6, 1929, Annie Webb Blanton Vertical File; Winegarten and McArthur, *Citizens,* pp. 219–30; Goad interview. In December, 1922, Blanton received a Christmas gift of $500 from the State Parent Teachers' Association as a token of its appreciation for her service as state superintendent, a gesture that indicated the group's awareness of her financial situation. (See Blanton to Cooper, Mar. 6, 1929, Annie Webb Blanton Vertical File.)

2. University of Texas President's File for Annie Webb Blanton; Blanton to Sutton, Mar. 14, June 15, 1923, HQ340, Sutton Papers; *Alcalde* 10 (Feb., 1923): 1859.

3. Blanton to Pennybacker, Oct. 14, 1923, 2M29, Pennybacker Papers (quote); Blanton, *Hand Book,* pp. 30, 191–99; Blanton to Sutton, Mar. 14, 15, June 15, 1923, HQ340, Sutton Papers.

4. *Handbook of Texas,* 2:692; Sutton Vertical File; Blanton to Sutton, Jan. 12, 1922, 2K330, Sutton Papers; Blanton to Sutton, Nov. 15, 1922, HQ339, Sutton Papers; Blanton to Sutton, Mar. 15, 1923, HQ340, Sutton Papers; Sutton to Blanton, Apr. 24, 1922, 2K330, Sutton Papers; Program for Conference Upon the Teacher-Problem in Texas, Apr. 21–22, 1922, 2K330, Sutton Papers; "Teaching as a Profession for Women," 2K331, Sutton Papers; Brown, *Hood, Bonnet, and Little Brown Jug,* p. 161; Campbell, "William Seneca Sutton," pp. 92–94, 141–42.

5. Blanton to Sutton, June 15, 1923, HQ340, Sutton Papers; Blanton, "A Study of Educational Progress in Texas;" Blanton, *Hand Book.*

6. Blanton to Sutton, June 15, 1923, HQ340, Sutton Papers.

7. Mrs. Lee Joseph to Sutton, June 23, 1923, HQ340, Sutton Papers; Sutton to Joseph, June 25, 1923, HQ340, Sutton Papers.

8. Blanton to Amon G. Carter, July 18, 1923, Amon G. Carter Papers, Southwest Collection, Texas Tech University; Jessie Daniel Ames to Carter, Aug. 3, 1923, Carter Papers. For more information on Ames, see Hall, *Revolt against Chivalry.* On the formation of Texas Tech and Carter's role as a regent, see Brown, *Hood, Bonnet, and Little Brown Jug,* pp. 142–44, 271–72.

9. Blanton, "A Study of Educational Progress," pp. 5–6, 324–25 (quote).

10. Ibid., p. 320.

11. Sutton Telegram to Pittenger, July 7, 1923, VF1/B, University

of Texas President's Office Records; Pittenger Telegram to Sutton, July 7, 1923, VF1/B, University of Texas President's Office Records.

12. Blanton to Sutton, Aug. 9, 1923, 2K332, Sutton Papers; Blanton to Pennybacker, Oct. 14, 1923, 2M29, Pennybacker Papers; information on school of education, 2K333, Sutton Papers; Blanton to Sutton, Aug. 20, 1923, VF1/B, University of Texas President's Office Records.

13. University of Texas President's File for Annie Webb Blanton; Blanton to Sutton, Aug. 20, 1923, VF1/B, University of Texas President's Office Records; Blanton to Pennybacker, Oct. 14, 1923, 2M29, Pennybacker Papers; Joseph to Sutton, Aug. 15, 1923, VF1/B, University of Texas President's Office Records.

14. Blanton to Pennybacker, Oct. 14, 1923, 2M29, Pennybacker Papers; Joseph to Sutton, Aug. 15, 1923, VF1/B, University of Texas President's Office Records; *Texas School Journal* 41 (Sept., 1923): 8.

15. Blanton to Pennybacker, Oct. 14, 1923, 2M29, Pennybacker Papers.

16. Reeda Lee Anderson, *A History of the College of Education of the University of Texas at Austin*, pp. 1, 38–39, 42–46, 52, 55–56; information on school of education, 2K333, Sutton Papers; *Handbook of Texas*, 2:692; *University of Texas Bulletin* 2417 (May 1, 1924): 198, 338; Austin Chapter, American Institute of Architects, *Austin: Its Architects and Architecture (1836–1986)*, pp. 40–41, 66. The three-story structure, built in 1918, was known as the Education Building until 1930, when it was renamed Sutton Hall in honor of the longtime dean. It housed the school (later college) of education until 1975. (See Margaret C. Berry, *The University of Texas: A Pictorial Account of Its First Century*, p. 70.)

17. Anderson, *History of the College*, p. 49; Blanton to Cooper, Mar. 6, 1929, Annie Webb Blanton Vertical File; *University of Texas Bulletin* 2417 (May 1, 1924): 198.

18. Pittenger to Splawn, June 8, 1925, VF1/B, University of Texas President's Office Records.

19. Various information on Sutton, 2K331, Sutton Papers; various correspondence pertaining to Blanton, VF1/A, VF1/B, VF6/C, VF26/D, University of Texas President's Office Records; *Handbook of Texas*, 2:692.

20. *Alcalde* 12 (Apr., 1924): 63; Blanton to Sutton, Mar. 15, June 4, 1924, VF1/B, University of Texas President's Office Records; Brown, *Hood, Bonnet, and Little Brown Jug*, pp. 142–44.

21. Blanton to Sutton, June 4, 1924, VF1/B, University of Texas President's Office Records; Brown, *Hood, Bonnet, and Little Brown Jug*, pp. 488–89.

22. Cott, *Grounding,* pp. 219–20, 227–28; Carter, "Academic Women Revisited," p. 680; *University of Texas Bulletin* 2417 (May 1, 1924): 342; *University of Texas Publication Catalogue* 4016 (Apr. 22, 1940): Part V, 91. According to these last two sources, the University of Texas faculty was 26% female in 1923 (seventy-five women out of 290 faculty members) but only 16% female in 1940 (ninety women out of 563 faculty members).

23. University of Texas President's File for Annie Webb Blanton; Brown, *Hood, Bonnet, and Little Brown Jug,* p. 167; various correspondence between Splawn and Blanton, VF1/B, University of Texas President's Office Records; C. H. Jenkins to Gen. M. M. Crane, Sept. 4, 1924, 3N106, Martin McNulty Crane Papers, Barker Texas History Center; *Handbook of Texas,* 2:670; Blanton to Pennybacker, Oct. 19, 1924, 2M51, Pennybacker Papers; Thompson, *Marking a Trail,* pp. 63, 69, 74.

24. Thompson, *Marking a Trail,* pp. 63, 69, 74. Throughout its history CIA had many prominent women board members, including Eleanor Brackenridge and Helen Stoddard. (See Thompson, *Marking a Trail,* p. 3; Winegarten, *Texas Women,* p. 99.)

25. University of Texas Memorabilia File, Barker Texas History Center; Ware, *Beyond Suffrage,* pp. 45–46; Ware, *Partner and I,* p. 184. The friends behind this campaign included University of Texas education professor Charles F. Arrowood, Houston principal Mamie S. Bastian, Waco school superintendent B. B. Cobb, San Antonio school superintendent J. C. Cochran, State College for Women (formerly College of Industrial Arts) president L. H. Hubbard, Austin school superintendent A. N. McCallum, and Texarkana school superintendent and Texas State Teachers Association president Henry W. Stilwell.

26. Blanton to Cooper, Mar. 6, 1929, Annie Webb Blanton Vertical File; University of Texas President's File for Annie Webb Blanton; Pittenger to Splawn, June 8, 1925, VF1/B, University of Texas President's Office Records; Anderson, *History of the College,* p. 47; various correspondence between Blanton and Pittenger, 4R26, 4R28, 4R29, Pittenger Papers.

27. Pittenger to Splawn, June 8, 1925, VF1/B, University of Texas President's Office Records; Blanton, "A Study of Educational Progress," passim. See also Smith, "Schools and Schoolmen," p. 38 for information on the problems in rural education prior to the twentieth century.

28. *Texas School Journal* 39 (Jan., 1922): 15; Pittenger to Splawn, June 8, 1925, VF1/B, University of Texas President's Office Records; Blanton, "A Study of Educational Progress," passim; Blanton, *Hand Book,* pp. 29, 36, 67, 69 (quote). See also Ellwood P. Cubberley, *The Improvement*

of Rural Schools for a discussion of rural school problems in a national context.

29. Splawn to Frank P. Bachman, May 13, 1926, VF1/B, University of Texas President's Office Records; Blanton to Splawn, May 18, Aug. 21, 1926, VF1/B, University of Texas President's Office Records; Blanton to Cooper, Mar. 6, 1929, Annie Webb Blanton Vertical File.

30. Blanton to Splawn, Aug. 21, 1926, VF1/B, University of Texas President's Office Records; Blanton to H. Y. Benedict, Jan. 2, 1929, VF1/A, University of Texas President's Office Records; various information on statewide educational survey, 2B61, Harry Yandell Benedict Papers, Barker Texas History Center; Annie Webb Blanton, "A Study of the County as a Factor in the Development of School Control," Ph.D. diss., Cornell University, 1927. The 1924 survey actually indicated that rural schools were in better shape than many Texas educators had believed. This result may have affected rural reforms at the public school level, but it did not change the university's plan for rural school training. (See Sitton and Rowold, *Ringing the Children In,* pp. 16–19.)

31. Blanton to Splawn, Aug. 21, 1926, VF1/B, University of Texas President's Office Records; Blanton to Pittenger, various letters, 4R26, Pittenger Papers; Splawn to Blanton, Aug. 28, 1926, VF1/B, University of Texas President's Office Records.

32. Blanton to Pittenger, Sept. 28, Oct. 22, 1926, Jan. 27, Mar. 5, May 12, Aug. 2, 1927 (quote), 4R26, Pittenger Papers; Blanton to Splawn, Sept. 19, 1926, July 12, 1927, VF1/B, University of Texas President's Office Records; Delta Kappa Gamma, *Pioneer Women Teachers of Texas,* p. 6; Blanton, "A Study of the County."

33. Blanton, "A Study of the County." The six states in the first group were Pennsylvania, Texas, Maryland, Nebraska, Louisiana, and Montana, and the second group included Alabama, Arizona, Iowa, Nevada, North Carolina, and Ohio. The dissertation topic she pursued was actually a replacement of an original idea to compare the activities of educators in one-teacher schools with those in graded schools. This topic would have required research by Blanton in New York schools, and it became impossible to complete after she suffered a severe case of influenza during Christmas, 1926, and found it too difficult to travel to various schools in snowbound weather following her illness. (See Blanton to Pittenger, Nov. 6, 1926, Jan. 11, Feb. 23, 1927, 4R26, Pittenger Papers.)

34. The quote is from Apr. 30, 1934, employment form in the University of Texas President's File for Annie Webb Blanton; University of Texas President's File for Annie Webb Blanton; *The Daily Texan,*

Oct. 30, 1945; University of Texas Memorabilia File; Delta Kappa Gamma, *Pioneer Women Teachers of Texas,* p. 6; Blanton to Cooper, Mar. 6, 1929, Annie Webb Blanton Vertical File; "Annie Webb Blanton Memorial Resolution," Annie Webb Blanton Vertical File. The university's Phi Beta Kappa chapter was not established until 1904, after Blanton's graduation, but she was selected as an honorary member while she was state superintendent. (See University of Texas President's File for Annie Webb Blanton; *University of Texas Bulletin* 2417 [May 1, 1924]: 45.) Lilia Mary Casis (romance languages) and Mary Edna Gearing (home economics) were the first two women to become full professors at the University of Texas. Casis began at Texas in the 1890s and Gearing in 1912. (See Berry, *University of Texas,* pp. 63, 73, 131, 137; Anderson, *History of the College,* pp. 42–43; Berry interview.)

35. Various information on Benedict, 2B60, Benedict Papers; various records on Blanton, VF1/A, VF6/C, University of Texas President's Office Records; Blanton to Benedict, Feb. 12, 1935, VF6/C, University of Texas President's Office Records; Benedict to Blanton, Feb. 15, 1935, VF6/C, University of Texas President's Office Records; *Handbook of Texas,* 1:146, 2:821–23. Rainey's controversial ouster in November, 1944, resulted in the presidency of T. S. Painter, with whom Blanton worked in a limited capacity for less than a year before her resignation and death in 1945. (See *Handbook of Texas,* 2:821–23; Rainey Controversy— UT Vertical File, Barker Texas History Center.) Pittenger served as dean of the school of education from 1926–1947. (See Berry, *University of Texas,* p. 161.)

36. Instructional Load, School of Education, Fall Semester, 1927, VF1/B, University of Texas President's Office Records; Blanton to Benedict, Oct. 15, 1928, VF1/A, University of Texas President's Office Records; Blanton to Pittenger, Feb. 2, 1928, VF1/A, University of Texas President's Office Records.

37. Blanton to Benedict, Jan. 2, Apr. 10, Aug. 1, 1929, VF1/A, University of Texas President's Office Records; Benedict to Blanton, Jan. 8, 1929, VF1/A, University of Texas President's Office Records; Blanton, *Hand Book,* p. 29. Blanton's involvement with the General Education Board and black education is discussed in chapter 3.

38. Blanton to Benedict, Aug. 1, 1929, VF1/A, University of Texas President's Office Records.

39. Teacher's Report 1929–1930, 4R103, University of Texas President's Office Records; Blanton to Benedict, Aug. 1, 1929, VF1/A, University of Texas President's Office Records; Blanton to Pittenger, Dec. 6, 1938, VF6/C, University of Texas President's Office Records.

40. Blanton, *Hand Book;* Annie Webb Blanton, *Advanced English Grammar;* Annie Webb Blanton File, The Woman's Collection, Texas Woman's University, Denton; University of Texas Memorabilia File; *Alcalde* 18 (Dec., 1929): 105–106; Brochure for *Advanced English Grammar,* Blanton Biographical File; Blanton to Sutton, June 15, 1923, HQ340, Sutton Papers; Blanton to Cooper, Mar. 6, 1929, Annie Webb Blanton Vertical File. *Advanced English Grammar* was referred to as an old but excellent grammar book in "Dialogue," *The Texas Observer,* Sept. 2, 1988.

41. Cott, *Grounding,* pp. 92, 94; Ruby Terrill Lomax Vertical File, Barker Texas History Center; Clara May Parker Vertical File, Barker Texas History Center, University of Texas, Austin.

42. Blanton to Mrs. E. H. Sellards, Feb. 24, Oct. 23, 1930, "Better Rural Schools for Texas—An Objective of the Texas Branches of the American Association of University Women" (by Annie Webb Blanton), "Rural School Research," "Dr. Blanton's Scheme for Studying Rural Schools to be Carried out at the University of Texas," "A Specific Instance—A Comparison of City and County School Administration," "Rural Conditions and the Rural Environment," "Plan for Study of One-Teacher Schools," all in MSS40, American Association of University Women Files, The Woman's Collection, Texas Woman's University, Denton. No concern for a fairer treatment of black schools, which suffered from both rural conditions and segregation, is evident in the particular reports above.

43. Blanton, "Better Rural Schools," MSS40, American Association of University Women Files.

44. "Rural School Research," "Dr. Blanton's Scheme," MSS40, American Association of University Women Files; Blanton to Sellards, Oct. 23, 1930, MSS40, American Association of University Women Files.

45. Annie Webb Blanton, *The Child of the Texas One-Teacher School,* p. 9.

46. "Rural School Research," "Dr. Blanton's Scheme," and Blanton to Sellards, Oct. 23, 1930, all in MSS40, American Association of University Women Files; Blanton to Pennybacker, June 21, 1931, 2M20, Pennybacker Papers; Blanton, *Child,* pp. 9–10. Blanton's replacement for her semester's absence was May E. Francis, who was a former state superintendent of education in Iowa. (See *Alcalde* 19 [Apr., 1931]: 240–41.)

47. "Rural School Research," MSS40, American Association of University Women Files; Blanton, *Child,* pp. 3, 5, 9–10, 11, 13.

48. Blanton, *Child,* pp. 25, 28–29, 44, 46, 67, 75, 95.

49. Various records on Blanton, VF1/B, 4R103, 4R104, University of Texas President's Office Records; Berry interview; Murray interview; McDermott and Kilgore interview; B. F. Pittenger, "Annie Webb Blanton," *Texas Outlook* 30 (Jan., 1946): 19.

50. Berry interview; Murray interview; McDermott and Kilgore interview; interview with Lorene Campbell, Austin, Sept. 22, 1989. Campbell worked for a brief time as a clerical assistant to Blanton in the 1930s at the University of Texas, typing correspondence for Delta Kappa Gamma.

51. Homer P. Rainey to Blanton, May 27, 1940, VF6/C, University of Texas President's Office Records; H. J. Lutcher Stark to Fred C. Ayer, July 30, 1940, VF6/C, University of Texas President's Office Records; Ayer to Stark, July 31, 1940, VF6/C, University of Texas President's Office Records; Blanton to Pittenger and Ayer, July 20, 1945, VF26/D, University of Texas President's Office Records. Ayer replaced Pittenger, who had become dean of the school of education, as chair of the educational administration department in 1927. (See Fred C. Ayer Vertical File, Barker Texas History Center; Anderson, *History of the College,* pp. 47, 63.) Stark's special interest in Blanton may have stemmed from the fact that his family was related to Blanton's brother-in-law, Frank Hill. (See *Handbook of Texas,* 3:922–23; information here also comes from the McDermott and Kilgore interview.) The Texas law mandating retirement for tenured professors who reach seventy years of age was repealed in the summer of 1989. (See *Daily Texan,* June 28, 1989; *The Chronicle of Higher Education,* June 28, 1989, A16.)

52. *University of Texas Bulletin* 2417 (May 1, 1924): 340–42; *University of Texas Publication Catalogue* 4016 (Apr. 22, 1940): Part V, 88, 91; *Handbook of Texas,* 2:821–23; Rainey Controversy—UT Vertical File; Don E. Carleton and Katherine J. Adams, "'A Work Peculiarly Our Own': Origins of the Barker Texas History Center, 1883–1950," *Southwestern Historical Quarterly* 86 (Oct., 1982): 224.

53. Parker Vertical File; Lomax Vertical File; Cora Merriman Martin Vertical File, Barker Texas History Center; Holden, *Our Heritage,* 1:18–19, 2:6; "A Tribute to Dr. Annie Webb Blanton," Annie Webb Blanton Biographical File; Berry interview; *University of Texas Bulletin* 2417 (May 1, 1924): 342; *University of Texas Publication Catalogue* 4016 (Apr. 22, 1940): Part V, 91.

54. Holden, *Our Heritage,* 1:18–19, 2:6; Flachmeier, *Pioneer Austin Notables,* 2:14; Blanton to J. W. Calhoun, Dec. 7, 1938, VF1/A, University of Texas President's Office Records; Blanton to Pittenger, Dec. 6, 1938, VF1/A, University of Texas President's Office Records; Ramsey

interview; visit to May Blanton Hill grave, Oakwood Cemetery, Austin, Mar. 1989.

55. Blanton to Splawn, Aug. 21, 1926, VF1/B, University of Texas President's Office Records; Blanton to Benedict, Aug. 17, 1928, VF1/A, University of Texas President's Office records; Barney, "The Congressional Career of Thomas L. Blanton," pp. 81, 103–104, 109; Brown, *Hood, Bonnet, and Little Brown Jug,* pp. 406–407; Winegarten, *Texas Women,* p. 114; *Daily Texan,* Oct. 3, 1945; *Austin American-Statesman,* Oct. 7, 1990; McDermott and Kilgore interview. The ultimate victor in the 1928 Senate race was Rep. Tom Connally. Thomas Blanton resigned his congressional seat to run for the Senate, but regained it in 1930 by defeating the widow of his 1928 successor. (See Brown, *Hood, Bonnet, and Little Brown Jug,* pp. 406–407; Barney, "The Congressional Career of Thomas L. Blanton," pp. 89–90.)

56. Flachmeier, *Pioneer Austin Notables,* 2:14; "Annie Webb Blanton Memorial," Dallas Independent School District, p. 14; *History of the Texas Federation of Women's Clubs,* 2:91, 106, 162, 164, 191, 230; J. S. Hardy to Sutton, Apr. 20, 1923, 2K331, Sutton Papers; University of Texas President's File for Annie Webb Blanton; Teacher's Report, Session 1927–1928, 4R104, University of Texas President's Office Records; Winegarten and McArthur, *Citizens,* p. 219; Benedict to Blanton, Sept. 6, 1932, VF6/C, University of Texas President's Office Records; *University of Texas Bulletin* 3941 (May 1, 1924): 186; *University of Texas Publication Catalogue* 4016 (Apr. 22, 1940): Part VI, 157; Hall, *Revolt against Chivalry,* pp. 62–63.

57. University of Texas President's File for Annie Webb Blanton; Holden, *Our Heritage,* 2:13; "Annie Webb Blanton Memorial Resolution," Annie Webb Blanton Vertical File; Blanton to Sellards, July 4, 1929, MSS40, American Assocation of University Women Files; Blanton to Splawn, Aug. 28, 1925, Aug. 21, 1926, VF1/B, University of Texas President's Office Records; Blanton to Benedict, Nov. 23, 1928, VF1/A, University of Texas President's Office Records; Blanton to Benedict, May 22, 1930, June 19, 1931, VF6/C, University of Texas President's Office Records; various teacher reports, 4R103, University of Texas President's Office Records; Blanton, *Hand Book,* pp. 75–76.

58. University of Texas Memorabilia File; Scott, *Southern Lady,* p. 230.

CHAPTER 5

1. *The Delta Kappa Gamma Bulletin* 3 (Nov., 1936): 50.
2. Holden, *Our Heritage,* 1:7. *Our Heritage* is the most comprehensive history of Delta Kappa Gamma and contains extensive informa-

tion about Blanton's life, both in and apart from the organization.

3. Parker, *Annie Webb Blanton, Founder,* pp. 11–12; Flachmeier, *Pioneer Austin Notables,* 2:14.

4. Seaholm, "Earnest Women," pp. 1, 4, 11–12, 184, 215; Blair, *Clubwoman as Feminist,* pp. 15, 57, 63, 93, 117–18; Scott, "The 'New Woman' in the New South," pp. 473–83; Scott, *Southern Lady,* pp. 158, 208; Winegarten, *Texas Women,* pp. 66, 100; Gammage, "Quest for Equality," pp. 18–19; Grantham, *Southern Progressivism,* pp. 202–204.

5. Winegarten, *Texas Women,* p. 100; Blanton to Pennybacker, Sept. 15, Oct. 26, 1917, 2M52, Pennybacker Papers; Blanton to Pennybacker, June 27, 1918, 2M57, Pennybacker Papers; Teacher's Report 1927–1928, 4R104, University of Texas President's Office Records; Joseph to Sutton, June 23, 1923, HQ340, Sutton Papers.

6. Scott, *Southern Lady,* p. 163.

7. Gammage, "Quest for Equality," pp. 14, 19. In the resolution passed at her death, Blanton's colleagues noted that she always had been a firm believer in "the efficiency of organization as an instrument for progress." (See "Annie Webb Blanton Memorial Resolution," Annie Webb Blanton Vertical File.)

8. Jackson, "Petticoat Politics," pp. vi–vii; Winegarten, *Texas Women,* pp. 105, 110, 116; Humphrey, *Texas Suffragist,* p. 5; Blair, *Clubwoman as Feminist,* p. xi; Cott, *Grounding,* pp. 23, 92, 97–98; Noralee Frankel and Nancy S. Dye, eds., *Gender, Class, Race, and Reform in the Progressive Era,* pp. 110, 122; George Brown Tindall, *The Emergence of the New South, 1913–1945,* vol. 10 of Wendell Holmes Stephenson and E. Merton Coulter, eds., *A History of the South,* p. 223. Nancy Cott notes that even though some women's clubs declined in the 1920s, such as the General Federation of Women's Clubs, others took their place, such as the Parent-Teachers Association. (See Cott, *Grounding,* p. 87.)

9. Cott, *Grounding,* pp. 89, 90, 92, 230.

10. Ibid., p. 231.

11. Cott, *Grounding,* p. 89. The quote is from Lena Madesin Phillips, the first executive secretary of the National Federation.

12. Ibid., pp. 90, 92.

13. Crawford and Ragsdale, *Women in Texas,* p. 196; interview with Theresa Fechek, executive director, Delta Kappa Gamma Society International, Austin, Nov. 11, 1986; *The Delta Kappa Gamma Bulletin* 10 (June, 1944): 25; Parker, *Annie Webb Blanton, Founder,* pp. 31–32; Holden, *Our Heritage,* 1:8, 19, 2:6; McDermott and Kilgore interview; Murray interview; "Annie Webb Blanton Memorial Resolution," Annie Webb Blanton Vertical File.

14. *The Delta Kappa Gamma Bulletin* 10 (June, 1944): 25.
15. Holden, *Our Heritage*, 2:9; *Texas School Journal* 37 (Oct., 1919), p. 9. In the *Texas School Journal*, Blanton's address to deans of women in the National Education Association entitled "Am I My Sister's Keeper?" is reprinted. It includes several references to the obligation she believed women had to the women who came before them and fought for equality.
16. Parker, *Annie Webb Blanton, Founder*, pp. 33–34; Delta Kappa Gamma, *Pioneer Women Teachers of Texas*, p. 6; Holden, *Our Heritage*, 1: 7–8; Berry interview; *The Delta Kappa Gamma Bulletin* 43 (Fall, 1976); Mary Beth Rogers, *Texas Women: A Celebration of History*, p. 63; various Blanton correspondence, MSS80, Delta Kappa Gamma Alpha State Organization Records, The Woman's Collection, Texas Woman's University, Denton.
17. *The Delta Kappa Gamma Bulletin* 37 (Fall, 1970); 43 (Fall, 1976); University of Texas Memorabilia File; Crawford and Ragsdale, *Women in Texas*, pp. 197–98; Holden, *Our Heritage*, 2:162.
18. "Annie Webb Blanton Memorial Resolution," Annie Webb Blanton Vertical File; Holden, *Our Heritage*, 2:19; *Our Golden Anniversary, Delta Kappa Gamma 1929–1979* (copy in Delta Kappa Gamma International headquarters, Austin); *The Delta Kappa Gamma Bulletin* 5 (June, 1939): 5–6.
19. *The Delta Kappa Gamma Bulletin* 5 (June, 1939): 6.
20. Interview with Phyllis Ellis, Fort Worth, July 14, 1988. Ellis, a longtime Delta Kappa Gamma member, and her housemate Eula Lee Carter were close friends of Blanton's in the latter years of Blanton's life. (See Holden, *Our Heritage*, 1:19.)
21. *The Delta Kappa Gamma Bulletin* 10 (June, 1944): 25. Of the three women who declined Blanton's invitation, Delta Kappa Gamma histories make reference only to Blanton's close friend and housemate, Clara Parker, who was a faculty member in the University of Texas school of education. Parker believed that because of the time constraints necessary for completion of her doctoral degree, she could not afford to join the organization in 1929; later she became an active member. (See *Our Heritage*, 1:8; *The Delta Kappa Gamma Bulletin* 5 [Jan., 1939]: 2; 10 [June, 1944]: 25.) Holden's *Our Heritage* (1:8) states that the three regrets were given because of other time commitments, lack of faith in the success of the proposed organization, and fear of criticism by male colleagues.
22. Holden, *Our Heritage*, 1:8, 2:19; visit to Anna Hiss Gymnasium, University of Texas at Austin, Aug., 1989; Program for the Delta Kappa

Gamma Society International Alpha State, Texas, Fifty-Ninth Annual Convention, June 16-18, 1988, San Antonio, p. 4; *Our Golden Anniversary;* Lomax and Martin Vertical Files; Berry, *University of Texas,* pp. 163, 184; letter to me from Texas State Teachers Association, Apr. 26, 1989; Better Schools Campaign Materials, Eby Papers. These sources include further information about the founders, none of whom is still living. Of the twelve, two held doctorates in 1929 (Blanton and Koch). All were single except for Odom (Martin was a widow and Terrill later married University of Texas faculty member John Lomax). Bastian and Williams were prominent members of the Texas State Teachers Association; Williams served as president of the association in 1921. She also served as secretary for part of the Better Schools Campaign that Blanton led in 1920. Koch went on to a distinguished career at the University of Chicago (1929–1950). Odom successfully fought for the right of married women to be allowed to teach in the Austin public school system. Hiss was actively involved in the construction of a gymnasium for women on the University of Texas campus in 1931 (it now bears her name). As did Blanton, Hiss had a controversial brother. In the 1930s and 1940s, her younger sibling Alger enjoyed a successful legal career in Washington, D.C., before Whittaker Chambers accused him of being part of a communist spy ring, resulting in Hiss's eventual imprisonment for perjury. (See John Chabot Smith, *Alger Hiss: The True Story,* pp. 4, 68, 180; Alger Hiss, *Recollections of a Life,* p. 1; *Austin American-Statesman,* May 31, 1989. Allen Weinstein, in *Perjury: The Hiss-Chambers Case,* also discusses Hiss and his family, but makes no mention of his sister Anna.)

23. *The Delta Kappa Gamma Bulletin* 5 (June, 1939): 5; 10 (June, 1944): 25. The initial name of the group was Kappa Gamma Delta, but when it was discovered that a national aeronautical fraternity already existed with that name, Blanton's group became Delta Kappa Gamma. (See Holden, *Our Heritage,* 1:7, 2:19.) The Faculty Women's Club near the University of Texas campus no longer stands; however, in 1989 a plaque was placed by Delta Kappa Gamma at 2610 Whitis to mark the site of the building where the organization had begun (visit to site, May 1989; Berry interview).

24. *The Delta Kappa Gamma Bulletin* 3 (Nov., 1936): 50.

25. Holden, *Our Heritage,* 2:138–39, 162; *The Delta Kappa Gamma Bulletin* 2 (June, 1936): 7; 3 (Nov., 1936): 50. *The Delta Kappa Gamma Bulletin* 43 (Fall, 1976) notes that Blanton and the eleven cofounders risked professional security and loss of employment because male educators disapproved of the group's founding. It is difficult to assess what the other

cofounders encountered in terms of criticism, but the written documentation in the organization's history offers no specific evidence of serious employment threats to them or Blanton. Blanton served as state president from 1929 to 1930 (there was not yet a national president) and then as national president from 1930 to 1933. (See Minutes, MSS80, Delta Kappa Gamma Alpha State Organization Records; Program for the Delta Kappa Gamma Society International Alpha State, Texas, Fifty-Ninth Annual Convention, p. 3.)

26. *Our Golden Anniversary;* Holden, *Our Heritage,* 2:6; Pittenger to Blanton, Mar. 28, 1938, 4R26, Pittenger Papers. For examples of approval on travel requests, see correspondence between Blanton and Pittenger, Blanton and Ayer, Blanton and Calhoun, and Blanton and Rainey from 1938 to 1945 in VF6/C, University of Texas President's Office Records. These requests indicated Blanton's increased travel as Delta Kappa Gamma continued to grow. She was careful to arrange her trips so as to have minimal impact on her teaching responsibilities, and her requests were usually approved with the stipulation that her classes be covered and the travel made at no expense to the university. Blanton also made arrangements through the university for clerical assistance for her Delta Kappa Gamma work. For example, Lorene Campbell, who had another full-time job with the university, typed letters for Blanton for a brief time in the 1930s (Campbell interview).

27. Pittenger to Rainey, Apr. 10, 1940, VF6/C, University of Texas President's Office Records.

28. *The Delta Kappa Gamma Bulletin* 5 (June, 1939): 13–14; 10 (June, 1944): 25; Program for the Delta Kappa Gamma Society International Alpha State, Texas, Fifty-Ninth Annual Convention, p. 2; Holden, *Our Heritage,* 1:19–20; *Our Golden Anniversary;* Minutes, MSS80, Delta Kappa Gamma Alpha State Organization Records.

29. *The Delta Kappa Gamma Bulletin* 10 (June, 1944): 26 (quote); Holden, *Our Heritage,* 2:19–20, 39, 139; *The Delta Kappa Gamma Bulletin* 2 (June, 1936): 7. By utilizing school superintendents and university officials around the country, Blanton indicated her willingness to take the advice of males in identifying potential members, although final acceptance of nominations was always left to Delta Kappa Gamma members. She realized, of course, that it was often only males who held the administrative positions necessary to evaluate classroom teachers.

30. *The Delta Kappa Gamma Bulletin* 10 (June, 1944): 26, 29; 15 (Summer, 1949): 22; Ellis interview; Flachmeier, *Pioneer Austin Notables,* 2:14; *Daily Texan,* Oct. 3, 1945; Holden, *Our Heritage,* 1:20, 2:140; *Our Golden*

Anniversary; Minutes, MSS80, Delta Kappa Gamma Alpha State Organization Records; University of Texas President's File for Annie Webb Blanton; letter to me from Birdella Ross, Aug. 11, 1988. Ross, a resident of Minneapolis in 1988, was formerly a national president of Delta Kappa Gamma.

31. *The Delta Kappa Gamma Bulletin* 3 (June, 1937): 12; 6 (Nov., 1939): 7; 7 (Jan., 1941): 21; 10 (June, 1944): 5; 43 (Fall, 1976): 3; University of Texas Memorabilia File; Crawford and Ragsdale, *Women in Texas,* pp. 197–98; Mabelle and Stuart Purcell, et al., *This Is Texas,* pp. 37–44; University of Texas President's File for Annie Webb Blanton; Teacher's Report 1936–1937, 4R103, University of Texas President's Office Records; Holden, *Our Heritage,* 1: pp. 20–21, 2:20; Delta Kappa Gamma, *Pioneer Women Teachers of Texas,* p. 6; Minutes, MSS80, Delta Kappa Gamma Alpha State Organization Records; Ellis interview. The lot referred to is at Twelfth and San Antonio in Austin and now is the site of the Delta Kappa Gamma International headquarters. Construction was delayed because of World War II, but the building was completed in 1956 and completely paid for before that time. (See Purcell and Purcell, *This Is Texas,* pp. 41–43.)

32. *The Delta Kappa Gamma Bulletin* 6 (Nov., 1939): 7.

33. Holden, *Our Heritage,* 2:10; Murray interview.

34. Holden, *Our Heritage,* 1:19 (quote), 22, 2:39–41; *The Delta Kappa Gamma Bulletin* 1 (Mar., 1935): 17; 1 (May, 1935): 6; 2 (June, 1936): 46; 5 (Jan., 1939): 6; 6 (Nov., 1939): 11; 7 (Nov., 1940): 16; 7 (June, 1941): 8–10; *Our Golden Anniversary;* Ellis interview; Blanton to Fannie Lu Yeager, Feb. 22, 1934, MSS80, Delta Kappa Gamma Alpha State Organization Records; Ramsey interview.

35. *The Delta Kappa Gamma Bulletin* 1 (Mar., 1935): 17; 1 (May, 1935): 6; Blanton to Yeager, Feb. 22, 1934, MSS80, Delta Kappa Gamma Alpha State Organization Records.

36. Holden, *Our Heritage,* 2:20.

37. *The Delta Kappa Gamma Bulletin* 3 (June, 1937): 13, 48; 5 (June, 1939): 6.

38. *The Delta Kappa Gamma Bulletin* 6 (Nov., 1939): 7.

39. *The Delta Kappa Gamma Bulletin* 10 (June, 1944): 4.

40. *The Delta Kappa Gamma Bulletin* 5 (June, 1939): 6.

41. Blanton's other activities are discussed in chapter 4.

42. Holden, *Our Heritage,* 1:21. See also *The Delta Kappa Gamma Bulletin* 8 (Nov., 1941): 12 for acknowledgment of Blanton as the stabilizing force of the organization.

43. Rainey to Blanton, May 23, 1940, VF6/C, University of Texas President's Office Records; Blanton to Rainey, Mar. 12, Sept. 5, 1941,

July 25, 1942, Mar. 19, 1943, Mar. 27, 1944, VF6/C, University of Texas President's Office Records; University of Texas President's File for Annie Webb Blanton; Teacher's Reports 1940–1941, 1941–1942, 4R103, University of Texas President's Office Records; Blanton to Pittenger, Apr. 21, May 1941, VF6/C, University of Texas President's Office Records. Blanton only rarely spoke of anything as interfering with her Delta Kappa Gamma work over the years. Occasional family illnesses interrupted some travel plans, and during the time she was carrying out her study of rural schools for the American Association of University Women, she slightly reduced her Delta Kappa Gamma activities. (See Blanton to Calhoun, Dec. 7, 1938, VF6/C, University of Texas President's Office Records; Minutes, MSS80, Delta Kappa Gamma Alpha State Organization Records; *The Delta Kappa Gamma Bulletin* 1 [May, 1935]: 7; 6 [Nov., 1939]: 10.)

44. Blanton to Rainey, Sept. 21, 1942, VF6/C, University of Texas President's Office Records; Purcell and Purcell, *This Is Texas,* p. 41; *The Delta Kappa Gamma Bulletin* 8 (Mar., 1942): 7; 9 (Jan., 1943): 13; Minutes, Annual Conventions, MSS80, Delta Kappa Gamma Alpha State Organization Records.

45. Holden, *Our Heritage,* 1:21, 2:6, 20, 140; Minutes, Annual Conventions, MSS80, Delta Kappa Gamma Alpha State Organization Records; Ramsey interview; *The Delta Kappa Gamma Bulletin* 10 (June, 1944): 4; "Are Tenure and Freedom Secure at the University of Texas," May 30, 1945, 4R22, Pittenger Papers. The country home outside of Austin, known as Grove House, is located near the community of Del Valle and is extant although in deteriorated condition, according to Ramsey, who is Thrasher's niece. Blanton had maintained a cordial relationship with Rainey, but there remains no record of her reaction to his firing, other than the signing of this petition. The petition represented an effort by some faculty members to reduce damage to the university, and it angered the pro-Rainey forces at the school. (See Carleton and Adams, "'A Work Peculiarly Our Own,'" p. 224.) Considerable information on the strained relationship between Pittenger and Rainey after Rainey's firing is available in 4R22, Pittenger Papers. Because Rainey was hired as president *and* as an education department faculty member, he thought Pittenger should retain him in the department after the regents fired him as president. When Pittenger left the matter to the regents, Rainey expressed bitter disappointment.

46. Blanton to Ayer and Pittenger, July 20, 1945, VF26/D, University of Texas President's Office Records.

47. Ayer to J. C. Dolley, Aug. 28, 1945, VF26/D, University of Texas

President's Office Records; Pittenger to Dolley, Sept. 1, 1945, VF26/D, University of Texas President's Office Records.

48. Standard Certificate of Death for Annie Webb Blanton; visit to Annie Webb Blanton grave, Oakwood Cemetery, Austin, Mar., 1989, where the family plot contains the graves for May and Frank Hill, Blanton, and Dorothy and Robert Thrasher, who died in 1986 and 1985, respectively; Holden, *Our Heritage,* 2:3; Will for Estate of Annie Webb Blanton, Travis County Clerk's Office; Will for Estate of Dorothy Thrasher, Travis County Clerk's Office. Blanton's death resulted in an interesting, although not unpredictable, controversy for her brother Thomas. After driving from his West Texas home to Austin for his sister's funeral, the former congressman wrote a scathing letter to Gov. Coke Stevenson complaining of the dangers he felt in making the drive in extreme darkness, as a result of strikes by electrical workers across the state. Noting that such darkness could lead to robberies, burglaries, and assassinations, Blanton urged the governor to mobilize the Texas Rangers and home guard, arm them with machine guns and other weapons, and let them run the labor saboteurs out of Texas. There is no evidence of a reply to Blanton from Stevenson. (See *Dallas Morning News,* Oct. 5, 1945.)

49. "Annie Webb Blanton Memorial," Dallas Independent School District, pp. 21–73; Minutes, Annual Conventions, MSS80, Delta Kappa Gamma Alpha State Organization Records; *The Delta Kappa Gamma Bulletin* 4 (June, 1938): 30; 5 (June, 1939): 5–6; 6 (Mar., 1940): 12; 6 (June, 1940): 17–19; 43 (Fall, 1976). The memorial booklet in the Dallas Independent School District records contains extensive details on memorials and letters Thrasher received upon Blanton's death. It was compiled by Blanton's friends, and a copy was given by Thrasher to the elementary school that was named for Blanton and dedicated in Dallas in 1956.

50. Holden, *Our Heritage,* 1:134–35; *The Delta Kappa Gamma Bulletin* 10 (June, 1944): 28–29; 12 (Nov., 1945): 31; *Daily Texan,* Jan. 9, 1955; interview with Fechek, Jan. 31, 1987, Austin; *Handbook of Texas,* 3:237; *San Antonio Light,* June 18, 1988. Numerous Delta Kappa Gamma scholarships of $2,500 annually are listed in Gail Schlachter, *Directory of Financial Aids for Women, 1987–88.*

CONCLUSION

1. "Annie Webb Blanton Memorial Resolution," Annie Webb Blanton Vertical File.

Bibliography

MANUSCRIPTS AND COLLECTIONS

American Association of University Women. Files. The Woman's Collection, Texas Woman's University, Denton.

Austin Independent School District. Employment Records.

Ayer, Fred C., Vertical File. Barker Texas History Center, University of Texas, Austin.

Benedict, Harry Yandell, Papers. Barker Texas History Center, University of Texas, Austin.

Blanton, Annie Webb. Biographical File, Austin History Center, Austin.

———, File. The Woman's Collection, Texas Woman's University, Denton.

———, Vertical File. Barker Texas History Center, University of Texas, Austin.

Blanton, Thomas L., Vertical File. Barker Texas History Center, University of Texas, Austin.

Bruce, William H., File. University of North Texas Archives, Denton.

Carter, Amon G., Papers. Southwest Collection, Texas Tech University, Lubbock.

Conference for Education in Texas. Records. Barker Texas History Center, University of Texas, Austin.

Crane, Martin McNulty, Papers. Barker Texas History Center, University of Texas, Austin.

Cunningham, Minnie Fisher, Papers. Houston Metropolitan Research Center, Houston Public Library, Houston.

Dallas Independent School District. Records. Dallas.

Delta Kappa Gamma Alpha State Organization. Records. The Woman's Collection, Texas Woman's University, Denton.

Delta Kappa Gamma Society International, Alpha State, Texas. Program, Fifty-Ninth Annual Convention, June 16–18, 1988. Author's collection.

Eby, Frederick, Papers. Texas Collection, Baylor University, Waco.

Ellis, Alexander Caswell, Papers. Barker Texas History Center, University of Texas, Austin.

———, Vertical File. Barker Texas History Center, University of Texas, Austin.

Fayette County Archives. Barker Texas History Center, University of Texas, Austin.

Hobby, William P., Papers. Archives Division, Texas State Library, Austin.

Hogg, William Clifford, Papers. Barker Texas History Center, University of Texas, Austin.

Legislative Committee to Investigate State Departments and Institutions, 1917. Archives Division, Texas State Library, Austin.

Lomax, Ruby Terrill, Vertical File. Barker Texas History Center, University of Texas, Austin.

McCallum, Jane Y., Papers. Austin History Center, Austin.

Marrs, Starlin Marion Newberry, Vertical File. Barker Texas History Center, University of Texas, Austin.

Martin, Cora Merriman, Vertical File. Barker Texas History Center, University of Texas, Austin.

Neff, Pat, Papers. Texas Collection, Baylor University, Waco.

Parker, Clara May, Vertical File. Barker Texas History Center, University of Texas, Austin.

Pennybacker, Mrs. Percy V., Papers. Barker Texas History Center, University of Texas, Austin.

Pittenger, Benjamin F., Papers. Barker Texas History Center, University of Texas, Austin.

Rainey Controversy—UT Vertical File. Barker Texas History Center, University of Texas, Austin.

State Department of Highways and Public Transportation. General Highway Map, Fayette County.

Sutton, William Seneca, Papers. Barker Texas History Center, University of Texas, Austin.

———, Vertical File. Barker Texas History Center, University of Texas, Austin.

Texas Department of Health, Bureau of Vital Statistics. Standard Certificate of Death for Annie Webb Blanton.

Texas Federation of Women's Clubs. Files. The Woman's Collection, Texas Woman's University, Denton.

Texas Historical Commission. Annie Webb Blanton Historical Marker File.

Bibliography

────. Asa Hill Historical Marker File.

Texas State Teachers Association Vertical File. Barker Texas History Center, University of Texas, Austin.

Travis County Clerk's Office. Will for Estate of Annie Webb Blanton.

────. Will for Estate of Dorothy Thrasher.

University of North Texas Academic Affairs Office. Files. University of North Texas, Denton.

────. Archives. University of North Texas, Denton.

University of Texas Memorabilia File. Barker Texas History Center, University of Texas, Austin.

University of Texas President's File for Annie Webb Blanton. Office of the Executive Vice President and Provost, University of Texas, Austin.

University of Texas President's Office. Records. Barker Texas History Center, University of Texas, Austin.

Woman's Shakespeare Club of Denton. Files. The Woman's Collection, Texas Woman's University, Denton.

DISSERTATIONS AND THESES

Barney, Bruce Lee. "The Congressional Career of Thomas L. Blanton." Master's thesis, Hardin-Simmons University, 1966.

Blanton, Annie Webb. "A Study of Educational Progress in Texas, 1918–1922." Master's thesis, University of Texas, Austin, 1923.

────. "A Study of the County as a Factor in the Development of School Control." Ph.D. dissertation, Cornell University, 1927.

Campbell, Phonsie. "William Seneca Sutton." Master's thesis, University of Texas, Austin, 1932.

Dawson, Irving Owen. "The Texas State Teachers Association: A Study in Public Employee Organization." Ph.D. dissertation, University of Texas, Austin, 1958.

Gammage, Judie Walton. "Quest for Equality: An Historical Overview of Women's Rights Activism in Texas, 1890–1975." Ph.D. dissertation, University of North Texas, 1982.

Jackson, Emma Louise Moyer. "Petticoat Politics: Political Activism among Texas Women in the 1920s." Ph.D. dissertation, University of Texas, Austin, 1980.

Nelum, Junior Nathaniel. "A Study of the First Seventy Years of the Colored Teachers State Association of Texas." Ph.D. dissertation, University of Texas, Austin, 1955.

Seaholm, Megan. "Earnest Women: The White Women's Club Movement in Progressive Era Texas, 1880–1920." Ph.D. dissertation, Rice University, 1988.

Bibliography

Smith, Stewart D. "Schools and Schoolmen: Chapters in Texas Education, 1870–1900." Ph.D. dissertation, University of North Texas, 1974.

INTERVIEWS

Berry, Margaret. Austin, April 1, 1989.
Campbell, Lorene. Austin, September 22, 1989.
Ellis, Phyllis. Fort Worth, July 14, 1988.
Fechek, Theresa. Austin, November 11, 1986, January 31, 1987.
Goad, Kay. Euless, July 14, 1988.
Kilgore, James. Dallas, September 9, 1988.
McDermott, Margaret. Dallas, September 9, 1988.
Murray, Betty. Harlingen, August 15, 1987.
Ramsey, Eugenia Hill. Austin, October 23, 1988.
Rogers, James L. Denton, February 13, 1987.

ARTICLES

Anders, Evan. "Thomas Watt Gregory and the Survival of His Progressive Faith." *Southwestern Historical Quarterly* 93 (July, 1989): 1–24.
Blackwell, Alice Stone. "Do Teachers Need the Ballot?" *Journal of Education* 70 (July 1, 1909): 8–9.
Carleton, Don E., and Katherine J. Adams. "'A Work Peculiarly Our Own': Origins of the Barker Texas History Center, 1883–1950." *Southwestern Historical Quarterly* 86 (October, 1982): 197–230.
Carter, Susan Boslego. "Academic Women Revisited: An Empirical Study of Changing Patterns in Women's Employment as College and University Faculty, 1890–1963." *Journal of Social History* 14 (Summer, 1981): 675–99.
Cott, Nancy F. "What's in a Name? The Limits of 'Social Feminism': or, Expanding the Vocabulary of Women's History." *Journal of American History* 76 (December, 1989): 809–29.
Duggan, Lisa. "Lesbianism and American History: A Brief Source Review." *Frontiers: A Journal of Women Studies* 4 (Fall, 1979): 80–85.
Gould, Lewis L. "The University Becomes Politicized: The War with Jim Ferguson, 1915–1918." *Southwestern Historical Quarterly* 86 (October, 1982): 255–76.
Graham, Patricia Albjerg. "Expansion and Exclusion: A History of Women in American Higher Education." *Signs: Journal of Women in Culture and Society* 3 (Summer, 1978): 759–73.
Griffin, Roger A. "To Establish a University of the First Class." *Southwestern Historical Quarterly* 86 (October, 1982): 135–60.
Lubomudrov, Carol Ann. "A Woman School Superintendent: What-

ever Happened to Mrs. McVicker?" *Utah Historical Quarterly* 49 (Summer, 1989): 254–61.

Moneyhon, Carl H. "Public Education and Texas Reconstruction Politics, 1871–1874." *Southwestern Historical Quarterly* 92 (January, 1989): 393–416.

Offen, Karen. "Defining Feminism: A Contemporary Historical Approach." *Signs: Journal of Women in Culture and Society* 14 (Autumn, 1988): 119–57.

Palmieri, Patricia A. "Patterns of Achievement of Single Academic Women at Wellesley College, 1880–1920." *Frontiers: A Journal of Women Studies* 5 (Spring, 1980): 63–67.

Pittenger, B. F. "Annie Webb Blanton." *Texas Outlook* 30 (January, 1946): 19.

Rupp, Leila J. "'Imagine My Surprise': Women's Relationships in Historical Perspective." *Frontiers: A Journal of Women Studies* 5 (Fall, 1980): 61–70.

Scott, Anne Firor. "The 'New Woman' in the New South." *South Atlantic Quarterly* 61 (Autumn, 1962): 473–83.

Sievers, Sharon. "Dialogue: Six (or More) Feminists in Search of a Historian." *Journal of Women's History* 1 (Fall, 1989): 134–46.

Weissman, Arnie. "Annie Webb Blanton." *Texas Outlook* 65 (Winter, 1981–82): 21.

BOOKS

Addams, Jane. *Twenty Years at Hull House.* New York: Macmillan Company, 1910.

Anderson, James D. *The Education of Blacks in the South, 1860–1935.* Chapel Hill: University of North Carolina Press, 1988.

Anderson, Reeda Lee. *A History of the College of Education of the University of Texas at Austin.* Austin, 1980.

Anti-Saloon League. *The Brewers and Texas Politics.* 2 vols. San Antonio: Passing Show Printing Co., 1916.

Austin Chapter, American Institute of Architects. *Austin: Its Architects and Architecture (1836–1986).* Austin: Austin Chapter, AIA, 1986.

Berkin, Carol Ruth, and Mary Beth Norton. *Women of America: A History.* Boston: Houghton Mifflin Co., 1979.

Bernard, Jessie. *Academic Women.* University Park, Penn.: Pennsylvania State University Press, 1964.

Berry, Margaret C. *The University of Texas: A Pictorial Account of Its First Century.* Austin: University of Texas Press, 1980.

Blair, Karen J. *The Clubwoman as Feminist: True Womanhood Redefined, 1868–1914.* New York: Holmes and Meier Publishers, 1980.

Bibliography

Blanton, Annie Webb. *Advanced English Grammar.* Dallas: Southern Publishing Company, 1928.

————. *The Child of the Texas One-Teacher School.* Austin: University of Texas, 1936.

————. *A Hand Book of Information as to Education in Texas, 1918–1922.* Austin: State Department of Education, 1923.

————. *Review Outline and Exercises in English Grammar.* New York: Charles E. Merrill Company, 1909.

————. *Supplemental Exercises in Punctuation and Composition.* New York: Charles E. Merrill Company, 1909.

Branda, Eldon Stephen, ed. *The Handbook of Texas: A Supplement.* Vol. III. Austin: Texas State Historical Association, 1976.

Bridges, C. A. *History of Denton, Texas from Its Beginning to 1960.* Waco: Texian Press, 1978.

Brown, Norman D. *Hood, Bonnet, and Little Brown Jug: Texas Politics, 1921–1928.* College Station: Texas A&M University Press, 1984.

Bullock, Henry Allen. *A History of Negro Education in the South from 1619 to the Present.* Cambridge, Mass.: Harvard University Press, 1967.

Calvert, Robert A., and Arnoldo De León. *The History of Texas.* Arlington Heights, Ill.: Harlan Davidson, 1990.

Chamberlain, Hope. *A Minority of Members: Women in the U.S. Congress.* New York: Praeger Publishers, 1973.

Clifford, Geraldine Jonçich, ed. *Lone Voyagers: Academic Women in Coeducational Institutions, 1870–1937.* New York: Feminist Press, 1989.

Conkin, Paul K. *Big Daddy from the Pedernales: Lyndon Baines Johnson.* Boston: Twayne Publishers, 1986.

Cott, Nancy F. *The Grounding of Modern Feminism.* New Haven: Yale University Press, 1987.

Cott, Nancy F., and Elizabeth H. Pleck, eds. *A Heritage of Her Own: Toward a New Social History of American Women.* New York: Simon and Schuster, 1979.

Crawford, Ann Fears, and Crystal Sasse Ragsdale. *Women in Texas: Their Lives, Their Experiences, Their Accomplishments.* Austin: Eakin Press, 1982.

Cremin, Lawrence A. *American Education: The National Experience, 1783–1876.* New York: Harper and Row Publishers, 1980.

Crutsinger, George M. *Survey Study of Teacher Training in Texas, and a Suggested Program.* New York: Teachers College, Columbia University, 1933.

Cubberley, Ellwood P. *The Improvement of Rural Schools.* Boston: Houghton Mifflin Company, 1912.

Bibliography

Delta Kappa Gamma Society, Alpha State Organization. *Pioneer Women Teachers of Texas.* Austin: Press of the Gannaway Print Company, 1952.

Dethloff, Henry C. *A Centennial History of Texas A&M University, 1876–1976.* 2 vols. College Station: Texas A&M University Press, 1975.

Eby, Frederick. *The Development of Education in Texas.* New York: Macmillan Company, 1925.

Eisenstein, Sarah. *Give Us Bread But Give Us Roses: Working Women's Consciousness in the United States, 1890 to the First World War.* London: Routledge and K. Paul, 1983.

Evans, C. E. *The Story of Texas Schools.* Austin: Steck Company, 1955.

Faderman, Lillian. *Surpassing the Love of Men: Romantic Friendship and Love between Women from the Renaissance to the Present.* New York: William Morrow and Company, 1981.

Faragher, John Mack, and Florence Howe, eds. *Women and Higher Education in American History.* New York: W. W. Norton and Company, 1988.

Flachmeier, Jeanette Hastedt. *Pioneer Austin Notables.* 2 vols. Austin: Privately printed, 1975, 1980.

Frankel, Noralee, and Nancy S. Dye, eds. *Gender, Class, Race, and Reform in the Progressive Era.* Lexington: University Press of Kentucky, 1991.

Geary, Linda L. *Balanced in the Wind: A Biography of Betsey Mix Cowles.* London: Associated University Presses, 1989.

Gould, Lewis L. *Progressives and Prohibitionists: Texas Democrats in the Wilson Era.* Austin: University of Texas Press, 1973; Austin: Texas State Historical Association, 1992.

Grantham, Dewey W. *Southern Progressivism: The Reconciliation of Progress and Tradition.* Knoxville: University of Tennessee Press, 1983.

Hall, Jacquelyn Dowd. *Revolt against Chivalry: Jessie Daniel Ames and the Women's Campaign against Lynching.* New York: Columbia University Press, 1974.

Harper, Charles A. *A Century of Public Teacher Education.* Washington, D.C.: National Education Association, 1939.

Haynes, Sam W. *Soldiers of Misfortune: The Somervell and Mier Expeditions.* Austin: University of Texas Press, 1990.

Hill, Lennon J., and K. Marie Watson Hill. *Isaac Hill, Sr. and His Descendants, 1748–1980.* Lubbock: Privately printed, 1980.

Hiss, Alger. *Recollections of a Life.* New York: Seaver Books, 1988.

History of the Texas Federation of Women's Clubs. 2 vols. Houston: Texas Federation of Women's Clubs, 1919; Denton: Texas Federation of Women's Clubs, 1941.

Hoffman, Nancy. *Women's "True" Profession: Voices from the History of Teaching.* Old Westbury, N.Y.: Feminist Press, 1981.

Holden, Eunah Temple. *Our Heritage in the Delta Kappa Gamma Society.* 2 vols. Austin: Delta Kappa Gamma Society, 1960, 1970.

Horowitz, Helen Lefkowitz. *Alma Mater: Design and Experience in the Women's Colleges from Their Nineteenth Century Beginnings to the 1930s.* Boston: Beacon Press, 1984.

Humphrey, Janet G. *A Texas Suffragist: Diaries and Writings of Jane Y. McCallum.* Austin: Ellen C. Temple, 1988.

Kessler-Harris, Alice. *Out To Work: A History of Wage-Earning Women in the United States.* New York: Oxford University Press, 1982.

Kraditor, Aileen S. *The Ideas of the Woman Suffrage Movement, 1890–1920.* New York: W. W. Norton and Company, 1965, 1981.

La Forte, Robert S., and Richard Himmel. *Down the Corridor of Years: A Centennial History of the University of North Texas in Pictures, 1890–1990.* Denton: University of North Texas Press, 1989.

Lerner, Gerda. *The Majority Finds Its Past: Placing Women in History.* Oxford: Oxford University Press, 1979.

Link, Arthur S., and Richard L. McCormick. *Progressivism.* Arlington Heights, Ill.: Harlan Davidson, 1983.

McComb, David G. *Houston: A History.* Austin: University of Texas Press, 1969, 1981.

McDaniel, Vernon. *The History of the Teachers State Association of Texas.* Washington, D.C.: National Education Association, 1977.

McKay, Seth Shepard. *Texas Politics 1906–1944, with Special Reference to the German Counties.* Lubbock: Texas Tech Press, 1952.

Members of the Legislature of the State of Texas from 1846 to 1939. Austin, 1939.

Monument Hill State Historic Site, LaGrange. Brochure, prepared by Texas Parks and Wildlife Department.

Parker, Clara M. *Annie Webb Blanton, Founder: The Delta Kappa Gamma Society.* Austin: Delta Kappa Gamma Society, 1949.

Pennybacker, Anna J. Hardwicke. *A New History of Texas for Schools.* Austin: Privately printed, 1888.

Peterson, Merrill D. *The Jefferson Image in the American Mind.* New York: Oxford University Press, 1960.

Pollard, Lucille Addison. *Women on College and University Faculties: A Historical Survey and a Study of Their Present Academic Status.* New York: Arno Press, 1977.

Public School Laws of the State of Texas. Austin, 1917.

Purcell, Mabelle, Stuart Purcell, et al. *This Is Texas.* Austin: Privately printed, 1977.

Rogers, James L. *The Story of North Texas from Texas Normal College, 1890, to North Texas State University, 1965.* Denton: North Texas State University, 1965.

Rogers, Mary Beth. *Texas Women: A Celebration of History.* Austin: Texas Foundation for Women's Resources, 1981.

Schlachter, Gail. *Directory of Financial Aids for Women, 1987–88.* Redwood City, Calif.: Reference Service Press, 1987.

Schmuck, Patricia A., ed. *Women Educators: Employees of Schools in Western Countries.* Albany: State University of New York, 1987.

Scott, Anne Firor. *Natural Allies: Women's Associations in American History.* Urbana: University of Illinois Press, 1991.

———. *The Southern Lady: From Pedestal to Politics, 1830–1930.* Chicago: University of Chicago Press, 1970.

Scott, Anne Firor, and Andrew MacKay Scott. *One Half the People: The Fight for Woman Suffrage.* Urbana: University of Illinois Press, 1975, 1982.

Sitton, Thad, and Milam C. Rowold. *Ringing the Children In: Texas Country Schools.* College Station: Texas A&M University Press, 1987.

Sklar, Kathryn Kish. *Catharine Beecher: A Study in American Domesticity.* New York: W. W. Norton and Company, 1973.

Smith, John Chabot. *Alger Hiss: The True Story.* New York: Holt, Rinehart and Winston, 1976.

Solomon, Barbara Miller. *In the Company of Educated Women: A History of Women and Higher Education in America.* New Haven: Yale University Press, 1985.

Tentler, Leslie Woodcock. *Wage-Earning Women: Industrial Work and Family Life in the United States, 1900–1930.* New York: Oxford University Press, 1979.

Thompson, Joyce. *Marking a Trail: A History of the Texas Woman's University.* Denton: Texas Woman's University Press, 1982.

Tindall, George Brown. *The Emergence of the New South, 1913–1945.* Vol. 10 of Wendell Holmes Stephenson and E. Merton Coulter, eds., *A History of the South.* 10 vols. Baton Rouge: Louisiana State University Press, 1947–67.

U.S. Congress. *Congressional Record.* 67 Cong., 2nd Sess., 1922.

Ware, Susan. *Beyond Suffrage: Women in the New Deal.* Cambridge, Mass.: Harvard University Press, 1981.

———. *Partner and I: Molly Dewson, Feminism, and New Deal Politics.* New Haven: Yale University Press, 1987.

Webb, Walter P., and H. B. Carroll, eds. *The Handbook of Texas.* 2 vols. Austin: Texas State Historical Association, 1952.

Bibliography

Weinstein, Allen. *Perjury: The Hiss-Chambers Case.* New York: Alfred A. Knopf, 1987.

West, Allan M. *The National Education Association: The Power Base for Education.* New York: Free Press, 1980.

Williams, Ruth Lynn. *Proudly She Serves.* Austin: Privately printed, 1976.

Winegarten, Ruthe. *Texas Women: A Pictorial History from Indians to Astronauts.* Austin: Eakin Press, 1985.

Winegarten, Ruthe, and Judith N. McArthur, eds. *Citizens at Last: The Woman Suffrage Movement in Texas.* Austin: Ellen C. Temple, 1987.

Woodward, C. Vann. *Origins of the New South, 1877–1913.* Vol. 9 of Wendell Holmes Stephenson and E. Merton Coulter, eds., *A History of the South.* 10 vols. Baton Rouge: Louisiana State University Press, 1947–67.

Index

Pioneer Woman Educator was composed into type on a Compugraphic digital phototypesetter in eleven point Baskerville with two points of spacing between the lines. Baskerville was also selected for display. The book was designed by Jim Billingsley, typeset by Metricomp, Inc., printed offset by Thomson-Shore, Inc., and bound by John H. Dekker & Sons, Inc. The paper on which this book is printed carries acid-free characteristics for an effective life of at least three hundred years.

TEXAS A&M UNIVERSITY PRESS : COLLEGE STATION